English Ab*u*sage

John Willard

English Ab***u***sage*
John Willard

Aerie Press
28 Patriot Street
North Andover MA 01845
johnwillard23@aol.com

Assistant Editors: Peter Beaven and Christian Waters

* Abusage-formerly immoral behavior, defilement. In later use frequently contrasted with usage. Abuse, misuse. Earliest use found mid-16th century.

Contributors:
Patrick Watrous, Matthew Villanueva
S. James Boumil III, Daniel A. LeClerc
Dr. Eugene Gross

Version 8.0 Revised: 7 October 2017

Published by
The Cheshire Press
an imprint of The Cheshire Group
Andover, MA 01810
www.cheshirepress.com

All rights reserved. No part of this book may be reproduced or transmitted in any form or by any means without the express written consent of the author, except for the inclusion of quotations in reviews.

Copyright ©2017 by Beaven & Assocites

ISBN: 978-0-9987465-7-9

Library of Congress: 2017948545

Printed in the United States of America

Beaven & Associates
3 Dundee Park, #202 A
Andover, MA 01810
978 475-5487
www.beavenandassociates.com

Willard, John
English Abusage

Contents

Introduction 8
  Correction Symbols 8
  Correction Practice 9
  Answers 11

Diction 12
  Diction I   1-20 13
  Diction II   21-40 15
  Diction III   41-60 17
  Diction IV   61-80 19
  Diction V   81-100 21
  Answers 23

Subject ≠ Verb Agreement 25
  Subject ≠ Verb I   1-20 27
  Subject ≠ Verb II   21-40 28
  Subject ≠ Verb III   41-60 29
  Answers 30

Misplaced Modifiers 31
  Modifiers I   1-15 33
  Modifiers II   16-30 35
  Answers 38

Two-Way Choice 42
  Two-Way Choice I   1-25 44
  Two-Way Choice II   26-50 46
  Two-Way Choice III   51-75 48
  Two-Way Choice IV   76-100 50
  Answers 52

Abusage 54
    Abusage I   1-15 55
    Abusage II   16-30 57
    Abusage III   31-45 59
    Abusage IV   46-60 61
    Answers 63

Proficiency 64
    Proficiency I   1–20 65
    Proficiency II   21-40 66
    Proficiency III   41-60 67
    Proficiency IV   61-80 68
    Proficiency V   81-100 69
    Proficiency VI   101-120 70
    Proficiency VII   121-140 71
    Proficiency VIII 141-160 72
    Proficiency IX   161-180 73
    Proficiency X   191-200 74

Mastery 79
    Mastery I   1-25 81
    Mastery II   26-50 83
    Mastery III   51-75 85
    Mastery IV   75-100 87
    Mastery V   101-125 89
    Answers 91

Challenge 93
    Challenge   1-25 95
    Answers 101

Practice Tests 102
Identifying Sentence Errors 103
   Identifying Sentence Errors I 104
   Identifying Sentence Errors II 106
   Identifying Sentence Errors III 108
   Identifying Sentence Errors IV 110
   Identifying Sentence Errors V 112
   Identifying Sentence Errors VI 114
   Identifying Sentence Errors VII 116
   Identifying Sentence Errors VIII 118
   Identifying Sentence Errors IX 120
   Identifying Sentence Errors X 122
   Identifying Sentence Errors XI 124
   Identifying Sentence Errors XII 126
   Answers 128

Improving Sentences 134
   Improving Sentences I 136
   Improving Sentences II 141
   Improving Sentences III 145
   Improving Sentences IV 149
   Improving Sentences V 153
   Improving Sentences VI 158
   Improving Sentences VII 162
   Improving Sentences VIII 166
   Answers 170

English Abusage

This battery of exercises is intended to improve prose through an exclusive focus on abusage. The book comprises some fifty-odd brief tests that rely on a shorthand of standard symbols used by editors and educators alike to mark faulty prose. Acquaintance with that symbology is introduced in the next few pages and aims at creating a reasonable readerly comfort level in progressing through this collection of error. The notations may serve as cautionary signposts of the customary pitfalls in English prose.

Introduction

These practice tests target abusage: the most common errors in English usage as defined by *grammar* — the rules for forming <u>correct</u> sentences — and by *syntax* — the conventions for making <u>sensible</u> sentences. The exercises are intended to issue warnings of prose missteps, to aid in recognizing abusage and offer preventive practice, and to promote, with mastery of usage, a confident writer.

This collection of abusage examples comprises a few dozen short-answer sets, best tackled in spurts, not in marathon sessions. The first practice group deals primarily with diction, the second with subject-verb agreement, followed by modifier mishaps needing longhand fixes. Subsequent exercises embed a variety of sentence errors that the reader is invited to identify using these:

Correction Symbols

case	(*nominative, possessive, objective*)	*p*	punctuation
<u>*c*</u>	capitalization	*pref*	pronoun agreement/reference error
comp	improper comparison	*ros*	run-on sentence, comma splice
d	diction, wrong word or part of speech	*sp*	spelling
frag	fragment; not a sentence	*s/v*	subject ≠ verb agreement
mm	misplaced or faulty modifier	*sub*	upside down ↔ subordination
nn	double negative	*t*	tense
#	number (*singular / plural*)	*ww*	wordy, redundant, tautological
//	parallel structure		
¶	paragraph	√	correct, ok

Correction Practice

Enter the proper error symbol or a √ in the blank.

_____ 1. A quiz show contestant is selected primarily on the single criteria of IQ.

_____ 2. Migratory birds typically fly South as the winter season approaches.

_____ 3. Everybody wanted to see the accident, the twisted wreckage was incredible.

_____ 4. The police had just arrived on the scene when she decides to start crying.

_____ 5. My sister is forever fiddling with her hair, which drives me crazy.

_____ 6. My European trip involved visits to capital cities, stops at famous landmarks, and using a rental car which broke down, plus side trips to tour art museums.

_____ 7. My friend was a fine guy, but I couldn't stand him driving.

_____ 8. He's not going to show up, I don't think.

_____ 9. When barely out of diapers, my mother put me in nursery school.

_____ 10. After my cousin and I had swum 20 laps, we were totally and utterly fatigued and felt wiped out.

_____ 11. Women more than men tend to be discrete about giving the ages.

_____ 12. A refugee boy reached out to catch a butterfly in the meadow when an anti-tank mine suddenly exploded in his face.

_____ 13. Neither my mother nor my father were able to help.

_____ 14. My brother had grown as big and heavier compared to as my father.

_____ 15. After a long, hot summer, having had our fill of the beach and ready to go home.

_____ 16. The troops slogged through the humid swamp they were plagued by mosquitos.

_____ 17. In the prison camps beatings were a daily occurrence.

_____ 18. The girl accepted a prom invitation with whoever asked her first.

_____ 19. My father's twin brother George retired from the Marine Corps in his early 50s.

_____ 20. On Thanksgiving, the President together with the First Lady traditionally issue a pardon to Tom Turkey.

Repeating, for reference:

Correction Symbols

case	(*nominative, possessive, objective*)	*p*	punctuation
c	capitalization	*pref*	pronoun agreement/reference error
comp	improper comparison	*ros*	run-on sentence, comma splice
d	diction, wrong word or part of speech	*sp*	spelling
frag	fragment; not a sentence	*s/v*	subject ≠ verb agreement
mm	misplaced or faulty modifier	*sub*	upside down ↔ subordination
nn	double negative	*t*	tense
#	number (*singular / plural*)	*ww*	wordy, redundant, tautological
//	parallel structure		
¶	paragraph	√	correct, ok

Answers

___#___ 1. A quiz show contestant is selected primarily on the ~~single criteria~~ ***criterion*** of IQ.

___c___ 2. Migratory birds typically fly ~~South~~ ***south*** as the winter season approaches.

___ros___ 3. Everybody wanted to see the accident ~~,~~ ***;*** the twisted wreckage was incredible.

___t___ 4. The police had just arrived on the scene when she ~~decides~~ ***decided*** to start crying.

___pref___ 5. My sister is forever fiddling with her hair, ***a habit*** which drives me crazy.

___//___ 6. My European trip involved visits to capital cities, stops at famous landmarks, ~~and using a~~ ***breakdown of a*** rental car ~~which broke down~~ , ~~plus we took~~ ***and*** side trips to ~~tour~~ art museums.

___case___ 7. My friend was a fine guy, but I couldn't stand ~~him~~ ***his*** driving.

___nn___ 8. He's not going to show up, I ~~don't~~ think.

___mm___ 9. When ***I was*** barely out of diapers, my mother put me in nursery school.

___ww___ 10. After we had swum 20 ~~tiring~~ laps, we were ~~totally and utterly~~ fatigued.

___d___ 11. Women more than men tend to be ~~discrete~~ ***discreet*** about giving the ages.

___sub___ 12. ***As a*** ~~A~~ refugee boy reached out to capture a butterfly in the meadow ***,*** ~~when~~ an anti-tank mine suddenly exploded in his face.

___s/v___ 13. Neither my mother nor my father ***was*** ~~were~~ able to help.

___comp___ 14. My brother had grown as big ***as*** and heavier ***than*** ~~compared to~~ my father.

___frag___ 15. After a long, hot summer, ***we had*** ~~having~~ had our fill of the beach and ***were*** ready to go home.

___ros___ 16. ***As the*** ~~The~~ troops slogged through the humid swamp***,*** they were plagued by mosquitos.

___sp___ 17. In the prison camps beatings were a daily ~~occurrance~~ ***occurrence***.

___√___ 18. No error: The girl accepted a prom invitation with whoever asked her first.

___p___ 19. My father's twin brother***,*** George***,*** retired from the Marine Corps in his early 50s.

___s/v___ 20. On Thanksgiving, the President together with the First Lady traditionally ~~issue~~ ***issues*** a pardon to Tom Turkey.

Diction

Simply put, diction deals with choice of words and, in speech, words' enunciation.

This set of written diction tests draws on frequently confused and misused words from the *Pitfalls* chapters in the companion book *English Usage*.

Diction I 1-20

The following exercise tests your familiarity with English words or phrases that may commonly be confused or misused, particularly in everyday speech.

____1. The protesters continued their march (<u>irregardless</u>   <u>irrespective</u>) of the consequences.
                                                      A   B

____2. Brussels sprouts taste quite different (<u>from</u>   <u>than</u>) their cabbage relatives.
                                                       A   B

____3. If one ever were to be captured, a unicorn would be a (<u>most unique</u>   <u>unique</u>) find.
                                                                       A   B

____4. Halfway through the race vs. the tortoise, the hare was considerably (<u>farther</u>   <u>further</u>) along.
                                                                                       A   B

____5. The car skipped over the curb and drove (<u>into</u>   <u>in</u>) the adjacent woods.
                                                         A   B

____6. Ernest Hemingway's 1942 war novel is (<u>entitled</u>   <u>titled</u>) *For Whom the Bell Tolls*.
                                                       A   B

____7. The ace student (<u>flaunted</u>   <u>flouted</u>) her *Phi Beta Kappa* academic achievement award.
                                A   B

____8. The legal dilemma in school segregation (<u>centered around</u>   <u>centered on</u>) equal opportunity.
                                                             A   B

____9. The attempt at humor in a time of tragedy is often viewed as (<u>kind of</u>   <u>somewhat</u>) sick.
                                                                              A   B

____10. A Marine wouldn't take an insult to his country (<u>laying</u>   <u>lying</u>) down.
                                                                  A   B

____11. The starving beggar desperately needed some passerby to (<u>loan</u>   <u>lend</u>) him a few dollars.
                                                                          A   B

____12. The reason for his absence was (<u>because</u>   <u>that</u>) he felt ostracized.
                                                  A   B

____13. Having heard odd noises, I looked around the garage, but everything seemed (<u>all right</u>   <u>alright</u>).
                                                                                              A   B

____14. The first prize being offered was over $500, and I was (<u>anxious</u>   <u>eager</u>) to win it.
                                                                         A   B

13

____15. Is there anyone in this big, old house (<u>besides</u> <u>beside</u>) me?
                                                                               A   B

____16. There is no doubt (<u>but that</u> <u>that</u>) the DNA fingerprint belonged to the accused.
                               A   B

____17. I was chosen to referee, given my (<u>disinterest</u> <u>uninterest</u>) in the outcome.
                                                  A   B

____18. My toddler (<u>brother</u> <u>brother's</u>) splashing in the mud was a laughable sight to behold.
                             A   B

____19. Not so much the candidates as the media (<u>decides</u> <u>decide</u>) elections.
                                           A   B

____20. After ballet class, the young girl complained that her arches were (<u>real</u> <u>really</u>) sore.
                                                                                                     A   B

Diction II 21-40

___ 21. (The fact that he succeeded   His success) was largely due to pure luck.
          A   B

___ 22. The agony of the marathon makes it a (torturous   tortuous) race for the runners.
                                               A   B

___ 23. My habit of pulling her hair as a tease always (aggravated   irritated) my sister.
                                                         A   B

___ 24. The deposed king was still beset by (allusions   illusions) of better days.
                                              A   B

___ 25. He was on time (as   like) he promised he would be.
                        A   B

___ 26. (Between   Among) the three of us we have just enough money to afford a dozen doughnuts.
          A   B

___ 27. The appearance of a white whale is a rare (phenomena   phenomenon) to behold.
                                                    A   B

___ 28. No one wants to attend the show (accepting   excepting) me.
                                          A   B

___ 29. With age, people begin to get forgetful of (alot   a lot).
                                                    A   B

___ 30. You will see I'm telling the truth if you look (in   into) my eyes.
                                                        A   B

___ 31. After mistakenly eating spoiled fish I didn't feel so (good   well).
                                                               A   B

___ 32. A good teacher shouldn't feel (badly   bad) about flunking an ill-prepared student.
                                        A   B

___ 33. From his mischievous grin, I (might of   might've) known he was up to something.
                                       A   B

___ 34. The washerwoman (hanged   hung) the clothes on the clothesline.
                         A   B

___ 35. The faulty old radiator let out an unpunctuated, (continual   continuous) humming noise.
                                                          A   B

____36. I (respectively   respectfully) decline your invitation to your wedding.
              A   B

____37. (Shall   Will) I go first or you?
          A   B

____38. Christopher Nolan is an (imaginary   imaginative) film director.
                                    A   B

____39. A pope is considered the most (imminent   eminent) member of the Catholic church.
                                          A   B

____40. The student (raised   rose) her hand.
                      A   B

Diction III 41-60

____41. Can a bribe (<u>assure</u>   <u>ensure</u>) a job-seeker employment in this administration?
          A   B

____42. Mimes often strike (<u>stationary</u>   <u>stationery</u>) poses for emphasis.
              A   B

____43. In hotels, a candy left on a guest's pillow is meant as (<u>complementary</u>   <u>complimentary</u>).
                                  A   B

____44. The (<u>capital</u>   <u>capitol</u>) of New York is Albany.
        A   B

____45. A quarter is worth (<u>less</u>   <u>fewer</u>) nickels than a silver dollar.
              A   B

____46. No (<u>amount</u>   <u>number</u>) of weaponry will suffice to vanquish the enemy.
       A   B

____47. A great number of jokes are aimed by married men at (<u>mother-in-laws</u>   <u>mothers-in-law</u>).
                                  A   B

____48. Preferring an antibiotic approach, the doctor was (<u>adverse</u>   <u>averse</u>) to removing tonsils.
                              A   B

____49. Staring into a kaleidoscope presents the eyes with colorful (<u>delusions</u>   <u>illusions</u>).
                                    A   B

____50. A poor housing complex in the inner city may be overcrowded with (<u>tenets</u>   <u>tenants</u>).
                                      A   B

____51. Meeting under the mistletoe at Christmas is supposed to (<u>assure</u>   <u>ensure</u>) a kiss.
                                   A   B

____52. Even well into the 20th century, many an outlaw was (<u>hanged</u>   <u>hung</u>) from a noose,
                                A   B

____53. Water as a rule boils (<u>in</u>   <u>within</u>) five minutes.
            A   B

____54. As a boy I was a next door neighbor of the (<u>Ames'</u>   <u>Ameses</u>).
                          A   B

____55. The sociologist found that the empirical questionnaire data (<u>was</u>   <u>were</u>) confusing.
                                      A   B

____56. It seems (<u>sort of</u>   <u>rather</u>) strange that bad guys always wear black.
              A   B

____57. It is considered good manners in the (<u>South</u>   <u>south</u>) to tip your hat to a lady.
                                              A   B

____58. My brother and sister are twenty and seventeen years old, (<u>respectfully</u>   <u>respectively</u>)
                                                                    A   B

____59. I should never have invited the salesman (<u>in</u>   <u>into</u>) the house.
                                                  A   B

____60. The passengers were shaken, but they are (<u>alright</u>   <u>all right</u>).
                                                  A   B

Diction IV 61-80

____61. The preacher assured his flock that virtually all of them in God's sight had done (good   well).
                                                                                    A   B

____62. You have done (badly   bad) by your cursing your parent.
                       A   B

____63. The official sent off the pair of athletes, saying "May the (best   better) man win!"
                                                                    A   B

____64. After the meeting ended, I asked the taxi driver to (bring   take) me home.
                                                             A   B

____65. The professor plunked down (8   eight) heavy tomes on the lectern.
                                     A   B

____66. By midnight the sitter (had   had had) enough of the toddler's tantrums.
                                A   B

____67. The reason I admired the book was (because   that) it was well written.
                                           A   B

____68. She excelled in sports played with a ball (;   :) tennis, soccer, softball, and field hockey.
                                                   A   B

____69. The ruby-throat is a just one (specie   species) of hummingbird.
                                       A   B

____70. If it (is   were) snowing now, then it's about time to go skiing.
               A   B

____71. My (two-year-old   two year-old) sister could count to ten.
            A   B

____72. The job seemed easy, but repainting the house took a (real   really) long time.
                                                              A   B

____73. My cat is (kind of   somewhat) shy around strangers.
                   A   B

____74. The bank pays a low rate of interest on the (principal   principle) invested.
                                                     A   B

____75. Neither my classmates nor the teacher (want   wants) to have a longer school day.
                                               A   B

____ 76. The teacher (rose   raised) the chalkboard.
                          A   B

____ 77. She's lost her mother, and I feel (bad   badly) for her.
                                            A   B

____ 78. I have (fewer   less) than five dollars in my pocket.
                  A   B

____ 79. It's a surprise party for our parents, so we must be (discrete   discreet) about preparations.
                                                                A   B

____ 80. Just about anyone in this room (might of   might've) ratted on you.
                                          A   B

Diction V   81-100

____ 81. The monster can't hurt you because it is (<u>imaginary</u>   <u>imaginative</u>).
                                                                              A   B

____ 82. A new policy will apply to all (<u>personal</u>   <u>personnel</u>) matters at the company, including
                                                                  A   B
promotions and vacation time.

____ 83. If the taxi will (<u>bring</u>   <u>take</u>) me to the post office I can mail the packages.
                                                 A   B

____ 84. The interest on the loan is five percent of the (<u>principal</u>   <u>principle</u>) per year.
                                                                                                  A   B

____ 85. All citizens must pay income tax, but that requirement (<u>accepts</u>   <u>excepts</u>) those under age 21.
                                                                                                              A   B

____ 86. I took care not to get anywhere near my flu-ridden friend's (<u>breathe</u>   <u>breath</u>).
                                                                                                                    A   B

____ 87. It's said that rats are the first to (<u>desert</u>   <u>dessert</u>) a sinking ship.
                                                                        A   B

____ 88. Before Salk's vaccine, polio was a disease that particularly (<u>prayed</u>   <u>preyed</u>) on children.
                                                                                                                  A   B

____ 89. Following the injury accident, the driver sought (<u>council</u>   <u>counsel</u>) from an attorney.
                                                                                            A   B

____ 90. I was undecided (<u>weather</u>   <u>whether</u>   <u>wether</u>) to accept pay for lending a friendly hand.
                                                   A   B   C

____ 91. The white-haired woman was a widow in her (<u>60s</u>   <u>60's</u>).
                                                                                           A   B

____ 92. She was amazed at the enormous (<u>amount</u>   <u>number</u>) of visitors that came to Florida.
                                                                          A   B

____ 93. The Dow Jones Industrial Average (<u>raised</u>   <u>rose</u>) today.
                                                                           A   B

____ 94. After enjoying a long weekend relaxing on the beach, I was (<u>loath</u>   <u>loathe</u>) to leave.
                                                                                                                  A   B

____ 95. The book title *All the King's Men* is an (<u>allusion</u>   <u>elusion</u>   <u>illusion</u>) to a children's rhyme.
                                                                               A   B   C

21

_____ 96. The doctor's promise of a speedy cure (<u>assured</u>   ensured   <u>insured</u>) her patient.
                                             A   B   C

_____ 97. In the springtime, when the air warms, a butterfly leaves (<u>its</u>   <u>it's</u>   <u>its'</u>) cocoon.
                                                                     A   B   C

_____ 98. A sidewinder snake leaves a (<u>tortuous</u>   <u>torturous</u>) trail in the desert sand.
                                        A   B

_____ 99. At the altar on the wedding day, the minister performed the marital (<u>rights</u>   <u>rites</u>).
                                                                                A   B

_____100. "Sour grapes" serves as the (<u>moral</u>   <u>morale</u>) of Aesop's fable about a fox's frustration.
                                        A   B

Answers

1-20

1. B irrespective
2. A from
3. B unique
4. A farther
5. A into
6. B titled
7. A flaunted
8. B centered on
9. B somewhat
10. B lying
11. B lend
12. B that
13. A all right
14. B eager
15. A besides
16. B that
17. A disinterest
18. B brother's
19. B decide
20. B really

21-40

21. B His success
22. A torturous
23. B irritated
24. B illusions
25. A as
26. B Among
27. B phenomenon
28. B excepting
29. B a lot
30. B into
31. B well
32. B bad
33. B might've
34. B hung
35. B continuous
36. B respectfully
37. A Shall
38. B imaginative
39. B eminent
40. A raised

41-60

41. B ensure
42. A stationary
43. B complimentary
44. A capital
45. B fewer
46. A amount
47. B mothers
48. B averse
49. B illusions
50. B tenants
51. B ensure
52. A hanged
53. B within
54. B Ameses
55. B were
56. B rather
57. A South
58. B respectively
59. B into
60. B all right

61-80

61. A good
62. A badly
63. B better
64. B take
65. B eight
66. B had had
67. B that
68. B :
69. B species
70. A is
71. A two-year-old
72. B really
73. B somewhat
74. A principal
75. B wants
76. B raised
77. A bad
78. B less
79. B discreet
80. B might've

81-100

81. A imaginary
82. B personnel
83. B take
84. A principal
85. B excepts
86. B breath
87. A desert
88. B preyed
89. B counsel
90. B whether
91. A 60s
92. B number
93. B rose
94. A loath
95. A allusion
96. A assured
97. A its
98. A tortuous
99. B rites
100 A moral

Subject ≠ Verb Agreement

Proper grammar insists that the *number* of the subject – singular or plural – must be matched with the corresponding number of the verb.

The rule is simple enough. But complication sets in: if the plural of a noun is not obvious, or the noun is spelled the same in both singular and plural, or in deciding grammatical priority between singular and plural compound subjects.

Subject ≠ Verb I   1-20

Select the letter of the correct choice.

1. ____ A high number of non-voting Americans (A. was B. were) in favor of an electoral recount.

2. ____ Neither one of the choices (A. seem B. seems) acceptable.

3. ____ Sixty-five minutes (A. was B. were) enough to decide the tennis match.

4. ____ The judge's sentencing criteria (A. are B. is) based on criminal intent.

5. ____ The physics of acceleration and momentum (A. involve B. involves) the use of calculus.

6. ____ The traffic data collected (A. was B. were) not enough to convince the mayor to widen the two-lane highway.

7. ____ A number of studies (A. has B. have) shown that drinking green tea promotes good health.

8. ____ The Navaho (A. is B. are) a people of the western U.S.

9. ____ Because of conflicting opinions, the jury (A. was B. were) unable to come to a verdict.

10. ____ Neither my parents nor I (A. are B. am) planning to attend the open house.

11. ____ Twenty dollars and twenty cents (A. was B. were) all my earnings for today.

12. ____ The lack of natural resources (A. has B. have) forced Switzerland to turn to banking.

13. ____ Courage differentiates cowards from (A. heroes B. heros).

14. ____ What we call "House Rules" (A. do B. does) not apply in professional games of poker.

15. ____ Good looks (A. is B. are) the basic qualification for a Miss America.

16. ____ Half of our group of twenty (A. are B. is) not here.

17. ____ He examined the scattered bones which (A. was B. were) once the skeleton of a squirrel.

18. ____ Under a high-powered microscope, bacteria (A. seem B. seems) enormous.

19. ____ The British Isles (A. is B. are) part of the European Union.

20. ____ The college faculty (A. has B. have) voted unanimously to admit women.

Subject ≠ Verb II   21-40

Select the letter of the correct choice.

21. ____ The wind damage from (A. tornados   B. tornadoes) can be severe.

22. ____ Neither I nor my friend (A. am   B. is) in the mood for an argument.

23. ____ Low octane gasoline coupled with Styrofoam (A. make   B. makes) a sticky napalm.

24. ____ IBM and (A. its   B. their) employees may not appear in corporate advertising.

25. ____ Semantics (A. deal   B. deals) with the meaning of words or symbols.

26. ____ Five and nine (A. is   B. are) fourteen.

27. ____ Neither snow nor sleet (A. amount   B. amounts) to weather deterring the U.S. Mail.

28. ____ An aspirin along with bed rest (A. are   B. is) the best recipe for a migraine headache.

29. ____ Either the annoying myna bird or the squawking canaries (A. need   B. needs) to go.

30. ____ Tony Orlando's singing duo, Dawn, currently (A. headline   B. headlines) in Vegas.

31. ____ Soft drinks or beer (A. go   B. goes) well with grilled burgers at a barbeque.

32. ____ Where I go to college is a decision my folks and I (A. am   B. are) unready to make.

33. ____ Neither one of us (A. want   B. wants) to be the first to say "good-bye".

34. ____ The statistical demographic data (A. are   B. is) inaccurate.

35. ____ Are pimentos just varieties of (A. tomatos   B. tomatoes)?

36. ____ Either dust or fumes (A. has   B. have) made it difficult to breathe.

37. ____ High IQ is not the most reliable (A. criteria   B. criterion) of common sense.

38. ____ Coffee and flapjacks or waffles (A. are   B. is) enough for breakfast.

39. ____ Four out of five dentists (A. recommend   B. recommends) sugarless gum.

40. ____ Whether the dorms or a sorority house (A. are   B. is) a better choice is hard to decide.

Subject ≠ Verb III   41-60

Select the letter of the correct choice.

41. _____ A sign indicated women's nightwear (A. was   B. were) on sale.

42. _____ Neither the visitors nor the home team (A. has   B. have) an advantage.

43. _____ Luggage, the sign warns, (A. has   B. have) to fit in the overhead compartments.

44. _____ The memoranda left for the babysitter (A. lists   B. list) the kids' chores and bedtimes.

45. _____ This sort of swearing and bad conduct (A. are   B. is) reprehensible.

46. _____ Three-of-a-kind (A. beat   B. beats) a pair in virtually all card games.

47. _____ Rabies, often carried by raccoons, (A. are   B. is) often fatal in humans.

48. _____ A fleet of paper aircraft (A. was   B. were) hanging from the boy's bedroom ceiling.

49. _____ Medical ethics (A. are   B. is) taught at a medical schools.

50. _____ Blue-fin tuna (A. is   B. are) now a delicacy, especially in Japan.

51. _____ At one time the Dallas Cowboys (A. was   B. were) considered America's Team.

52. _____ Electronic junk heaps are littered with obsolete (A. PCs   B. PC's).

53. _____ While the sorts of jungle illness (A. varies   B. vary), antibiotics provide answers.

54. _____ This route as well as the adjacent ones (A. lead   B. leads) toward the city.

55. _____ Vermin (A. have   B. has) infested the dank cellar.

56. _____ My boss along with his intern (A. attend   B. attends) monthly sales meetings.

57. _____ The woman's beloved and precious jewelry (A. was   B. were) stolen.

58. _____ Submarines are armed with lethal (A. torpedos   B. torpedoes).

59. _____ A barbershop quartet (A. make   B. makes) harmonious music.

60. _____ He bet his last dollar on the roll of a single (A. die   B. dice).

Answers

1. was
2. seems
3. was
4. are
5. involves
6. were
7. have
8. is
9. were
10. am
11. was
12. has
13. heroes
14. does
15. are
16. are
17. were
18. seem
19. is
20. has
21. tornadoes
22. is
23. makes
24. its
25. deals
26. is
27. amounts
28. is
29. need
30. headlines
31. goes
32. are
33. wants
34. are
35. tomatoes
36. have
37. criterion
38. are
39. recommend
40. is
41. was
42. has
43. has
44. list
45. is
46. beats
47. is
48. was
49. is
50. is
51. was
52. PCs
53. vary
54. leads
55. have
56. attends
57. was
58. torpedoes
59. makes
60. die

Misplaced Modifiers

Modifiers are those words, phrases, or clauses which describe and so limit or restrict the meaning of nouns or pronouns. Modifiers may be adverbs, adjectives, verbs, prepositional phrases, or their forms, but may not themselves be substantives: (non-possessive) nouns may not modify nouns.

In a sentence, modifiers belong next to, or as close as possible to, their objects of modification. Misplaced modifiers are those not located immediately near their objects, having ambiguous objects, or left dangling without an object. A related and inverse difficulty is a pronoun without a referent noun.

Modifiers I   1-15

Repair the following sentences. Answers may vary.

1. We don't sell lemonade to anyone in glasses.

2. To be admitted to an Ivy League school, grades had to be exceptional.

3. Between a rock and a hard place is where either choice looks bad.

4. Chicken Little encounters Foxy Loxy still shrieking "the sky is falling".

5. The general announced at daybreak the troops would face the enemy.

6. What he meant to say was uncertain.

7. Snake eyes is when you get two ones rolling the dice.

8. The reason for Mother's anger was because, looking at my room, I'd left a mess.

9. After filling up, the bus proceeded on its way.

10. Walter Mitty pictured himself as a surgeon with great expectations.

11. While tapping a message on his cell phone, his car skidded into a ditch.

12. Lifting weights rapidly strengthens arm muscles.

13. A Mexican stand-off in a confrontation is when neither side can win.

14. It says on the play-off roster that our team plays first.

15. The astronomer observed the rings of Saturn seated at his telescope.

Modifiers II 16-30

*The correction symbols "**mm**" and "**pref**" designate mistaken (mm), vague, or non-existent (pref) referents. This exercise asks you to write longhand responses.*

16. The following sentence may have *five* different meanings, depending on where the word "only" is inserted *mm*. Write three variations:

    Visitors can walk in the restricted area.

    A.

    B.

    C.

17. Rewrite the following sentence to yield two discrete meanings when the word "hot" is inserted:

    The waitress served a cup of tea.

    A.

    B.

18. Similarly, depending on the position of modifiers or referents, sentences may be understood in two ways. Rewrite or reconstruct the following **two-way modifier** sentences to disambiguate them.

    My mother told me on Monday to stay home.

    A.

    B.

19.   ***I dropped the pitcher on the table and it broke.***

    A.

    B.

20. This next one is tough to remedy unless you make assumptions about reasons and locations. Think about it! (For this example fill in your own details.)

   The police told the residents that they had to leave.

   _____

   _____

Other kinds of misplaced modifiers involve a **dangling** or mistaken referent. *mm pref*

21. *Buzzing near my head, my ears detected a swarm of bees.*

   _____

   _____

22. *When buying a phone, the variety can be overwhelming.*

   _____

   _____

23. *Inhaling secondhand smoke, statistics show is often as bad as smoking.*

   _____

   _____

Further examples of misplaced modifiers can have slightly comic effects. *mm pref*

24. *The weatherman said it's going to snow on TV.*

   _____

25. *My pal said he had visited Europe during intermission.*

_____

26. *A swimsuit model posed with the lifeguard in a bikini.*

_____

A related modifier error is a type of *pref* or improper or vague pronoun referent error which occurs if a pronoun has no discrete substantive that **it** refers to. Reconstruct the following "pref" error sentences.

27. *It says on the map where we need to turn.*

_____

28. *She was musically talented but had no chance to use it.*

_____

29. *If she makes it on Broadway, she'll be a big star.*

_____

30. *It's raining outside.*

_____

Answers

Note: Answers may vary.

Exercise 1:

1. *We sell no lemonade to anyone who wears glasses.*

2. *Exceptional grades are required of a student seeking admission to an Ivy League school.*
   To be admitted to an Ivy League school, an applicant needs exceptional grades.

3. *"Between a rock and a hard place" characterizes a choice of two bad alternatives.*
   Having two bad choices means being between a rock and a hard place.

4. *Still shrieking "the sky is falling", Chicken Little encounters Foxy Loxy.*
   Chicken Little is still shrieking "the sky is falling" when he encounters Foxy Loxy.

5. *At daybreak the general announced that the troops would face the enemy.*
   or:
   The general announced that the troops would face the enemy at daybreak.

6. *What he said contained not a bit of truth.*
   Not a bit of truth was in what he said.

7. *Snakes eyes is a dice roll of double ones.*
   Rolling two ones on the dice is known as snake eyes.

8. *My Mother was angry at my leaving my room a mess.*
   Seeing that I'd left my room a mess, Mother was angry.
   The reason for Mother's anger was that I'd left my room a mess.

9. *Once its gas tank was filled, the bus proceeded on its way.*
   The bus proceeded on its way after it filled up with passengers,

10. *With great expectations, Walter Mitty pictured himself as a surgeon.*
    Walter Mitty pictured himself as a surgeon filled with great expectations.
    Walter Mitty pictured himself full of great expectations as a surgeon.

11. *While tapping a message on his cell phone, the driver felt his car skid into a ditch.*
    A car skidded into a ditch while its driver was tapping a message on his cell phone.

12. *Rapid lifting of weights strengthens arm muscles.*
    Lifting weights strengthens arm muscles rapidly.

13. *A Mexican stand-off is a confrontation in which neither side can win.*
    A confrontation in which neither side can win is a Mexican stand-off.

14. *According to the play-off roster our team plays first.*
    Our team plays first according to the play-off roster.

15. *Seated at his telescope, the astronomer observed the rings of Saturn.*

Exercise 2:

16.
<u>Only</u> *visitors can walk in the restricted area.*
Visitors <u>only</u> can walk in the restricted area.
Visitors can <u>only</u> walk in the restricted area.
Visitors can walk <u>only</u> in the restricted area.
Visitors can walk in the <u>only</u> restricted area.
Visitors can walk in the restricted <u>only</u> area.
Visitors can walk in the restricted area <u>only</u>.

17.
The waitress served a <u>hot</u> cup of tea.   or
The waitress served a cup of <u>hot</u> tea.
                and
The <u>hot</u> waitress served a cup of tea.

18.
<u>On</u> <u>Monday</u> *my mother told me to stay home.*   or
My mother <u>on</u> <u>Monday</u> told me to stay home.
                and
My mother told me to stay home <u>on</u> <u>Monday</u>.

19.
I dropped the pitcher on the table, and <u>the</u> <u>pitcher</u> broke.   or
I dropped the pitcher on the table, and <u>the</u> <u>table</u> broke.

20.
The police ordered the residents to leave.   or
Saying duty elsewhere compelled them to leave, the police told the residents to depart.   or
The police needed to leave, and they so informed the residents.

21.
My ears detected a swarm of bees buzzing near my head.   or
Buzzing near my head I detected a swarm of bees.   or
I heard a swarm of bees buzzing near my head.

22.
The variety of phones for sale can be overwhelming. or
A would-be purchaser may find the variety of phones overwhelming. or
The variety of phones may be overwhelming to a buyer.

23.
Statistics show that inhaling secondhand smoke is often as bad as smoking. or
Inhaling secondhand smoke, as statistics show, is often as bad as smoking.

24.
The weatherman on TV said it's going to snow. or
The TV weatherman said it's going to snow.

But **not**: *x* *On the TV the weatherman said it's going to snow. [Why not?]*

25.
My pal said during intermission that he had visited Europe. or
During intermission my pal said that he had visited Europe.

26.
A swimsuit model in a bikini posed with the lifeguard.

27.
The map shows *where we need to turn.*

28.
She was musically talented but had no chance to use that talent. or
She had musical talent but had no chance to use it.

29.
If she succeeds on Broadway, she'll be a big star. or
If she is successful on Broadway, she'll be a big star.

30.
Rain is falling.

Two-Way Choice

Here begins the first of multiple practice sets that use the standard Correction Symbols. The choices in these exercises are bipolar but not necessarily obvious.

For convenience, the end of the *English Usage* text contains cross reference listing each correction symbol and corresponding pages discussing the error and its remediation.

Two-Way Choice

Select the underlined option to make the sentence correct and supply the symbol naming the error.

Correction Symbols

case	(*nominative, possessive, objective*)	**p**	punctuation
c̲	capitalization	**pref**	pronoun agreement/reference error
comp	improper comparison	**ros**	run-on sentence, comma splice
d	diction, wrong word, part of speech	**sp**	spelling
frag	fragment; not a sentence	**s/v**	subject ≠ verb agreement
mm	misplaced or faulty modifier	**sub**	upside down ↔ subordination
nn	double negative	**t**	tense
#	number (*singular / plural*)	**ww**	wordy, repetitive, tautological
¶	paragraph		
//	parallel structure	**√**	correct, ok

The following ten examples and answers demonstrate how to proceed:

_____ 1. Right next door to the (<u>Jones'</u> <u>Joneses</u>) lived a family named Smith.
                                       A   B

B case   **(should be objective not possessive)**

_____ 2. By midnight, I (<u>lay</u> <u>had lain</u>) awake in bed for two hours.
                            C   D

D t   **(past perfect not perfect tense)**

_____ 3. As his high school's valedictorian, (<u>the rejection letter stunned the boy</u>
                                                            F

the boy was stunned by the Harvard rejection letter).
                        G

G mm   **("valedictorian" should be modified by "boy" not "letter")**

_____ 4. Both the French and American flags are (<u>red, white and blue</u>   <u>red, white, and blue</u>).
                                                          A   B

B p   **(members of a series of three or more are set off by commas)**

_____ 5. The marriage was not only hasty but (<u>also</u>) an ill-advised pairing (<u>as well</u>).
                                                                      C   D

C comp   **(the comparative pairing should be "not only...but also")**

_____ 6. The hero, Peter Pan, together with the Lost Boys (<u>lives</u> <u>live</u>) in Neverland.
                                                                                      F   G

F s/v   **(singular subject takes singular verb)**

_____ 7. (<u>In the past</u>) I think it's clear that (<u>historically</u>) tyranny is eventually overthrown.
                           A   B

B ww   **(tautology: in the past/ history shows)**

_____ 8. He swore that he didn't now, <u>nor</u> at any prior time, do <u>nothing</u> wrong.
                                                        G   H

G nn   **("nothing" is a double negative)**

_____ 9. After hiking (<u>North</u> <u>north</u>) five miles, they sat and rested.
                                      A   B

B c   **(lower case direction indicates compass point not place)**

_____ 10. Reuben sandwiches are a (<u>really</u> <u>real</u>) tasty treat.
                                                 C   D

C d   **(a modifying adverb not adjective is called for)**

Two-Way Choice I 1-25

case	(*nominative, possessive, objective*)	**p**	punctuation
c	capitalization	**pref**	pronoun agreement/reference error
comp	improper comparison	**ros**	run-on sentence, comma splice
d	diction, wrong word, part of speech	**sp**	spelling
frag	fragment; not a sentence	**s/v**	subject ≠ verb agreement
mm	misplaced or faulty modifier	**sub**	upside down ↔ subordination
nn	double negative	**t**	tense
#	number (*singular / plural*)	**ww**	wordy, repetitive, tautological
¶	paragraph		
//	parallel structure	**√**	correct, ok

_____ 1. After the rain has stopped, the man (<u>closes</u>   <u>had closed</u>) his umbrella.
                                                                A   B

_____ 2. Tykes like playing tag, <u>to blow out birthday candles</u>, and <u>ripping open gifts</u>.
                                                                             C   D

_____ 3. You (<u>should of</u>   <u>should've</u>) seen her face when her fiancé appeared.
                                          A   B

_____ 4. She <u>won't be leaving</u> the hospital any time soon, given her illness, I <u>don't think</u>.
                                  C   D

_____ 5. I think I'd be successful leading troops if I (<u>was</u>   <u>were</u>) an army commander.
                                                                                                                  A   B

_____ 6. English is spoken differently in Scotland (<u>from</u>   <u>than</u>) in Wales.
                                                                                    C   D

_____ 7. The prize goes to (<u>whoever</u>   <u>whomever</u>) is first across the finish line.
                                                             A   B

_____ 8. Without a map, I can't help (<u>but wonder</u>   <u>wondering</u>) where I'm at.
                                                                   C   D

_____ 9. There's no one home but (<u>we</u>   <u>us</u>) children.
                                                          A B

_____ 10. The grandniece received a bequest from her (<u>belated</u>   <u>late</u>) uncle.
                                                                             C   D

_____ 11. <u>One</u> should always look both ways before <u>you</u> cross the street or railroad tracks.
                       D   F

_____ 12. We haven't enough train fare money (<u>among</u> <u>between</u>) poor both of us.
                                                      A   B

_____ 13. There (<u>seems</u> <u>seem</u>) to be several missing from my desk drawer.
                       F   G

_____ 14. Her skill in yoga, tai chi, gymnastics, and martial arts (<u>prove</u> <u>proves</u>) her agility.
                                                                         A   B

_____ 15. I (<u>definitely</u> <u>definately</u>) have enough money to afford a new car.
                   C   D

_____ 16. Cruel Hitler (<u>hanged</u> <u>hung</u>) presumed traitors with piano wire.
                              A   B

_____ 17. There's no doubt it was (<u>we</u> <u>us</u>) who were to blame for the fiasco.
                                         C   D

_____ 18. <u>The reason</u> why I put the dog on a diet is <u>because</u> he was far too fat.
                    F   G

_____ 19. A hung jury (<u>has</u> <u>have</u>) no uniform decision as to the defendant's guilt or innocence.
                            A   B

_____ 20. Neither you nor your friend (<u>want</u> <u>wants</u>) to become a victim of foul play.
                                             C   D

_____ 21. <u>On entering the dining room,</u> <u>the wine cellar is immediately below you</u>.
                         F   G

_____ 22. (<u>With</u> <u>Without</u>) scarcely a sound, we crept into the rat infested basement.
                  A   B

_____ 23. There can be no question but (<u>what</u> <u>that</u>) he's the jolly good fellow.
                                              C   D

_____ 24. Yesterday I read the notice where it (<u>fell</u> <u>had fallen</u>) on the floor.
                                                     F   G

_____ 25. I should have preferred to (<u>have sat</u> <u>sit</u>) in the balcony, not the front row.
                                            A   B

Two-Way Choice II 26-50

case	(*nominative, possessive, objective*)	**p**	punctuation
c	capitalization	**pref**	pronoun agreement/reference error
comp	improper comparison	**ros**	run-on sentence, comma splice
d	diction, wrong word, part of speech	**sp**	spelling
frag	fragment; not a sentence	**s/v**	subject ≠ verb agreement
mm	misplaced or faulty modifier	**sub**	upside down ↔ subordination
nn	double negative	**t**	tense
#	number (*singular / plural*)	**ww**	wordy, repetitive, tautological
¶	paragraph		
//	parallel structure	**√**	correct, ok

_____ 26. Walking down the hill, (a sink hole came into our view   we saw a sinkhole).
                                                                                C   D

_____ 27. If I (had known   knew) you'd be late, I'd have left home later.
                                  F   G

_____ 28. I owe this black eye to my twin (brother   brother,) Ralph.
                                                          A   B

_____ 29. I rode my bike for a mile around the neighborhood and (only fell   fell only) once.
                                                                                            C   D

_____ 30. (In my wallet) I counted just nine dollars. I counted just nine dollars (in my wallet).
                            F   G

_____ 31. The boss disapproves of (me   my) fiddling with my cell phone in the office.
                                                            A   B

_____ 32. The detective found the corpse (laying   lying) sprawled on the floor.
                                                         C   D

_____ 33. (Who   Whom) is to be elected the next school board president?
                              F   G

_____ 34. (A cow kicked over a lantern, thus causing the Great Chicago Fire.)
                            A
                   (The Great Chicago Fire ensued when a cow kicked over a lantern.)
                            B

_____ 35. The man in black is the one (who's   whose) accent is Bostonian.
                                                C   D

_____ 36. Besides talent, what (was   were) the other judgment criteria?
                                       A   B

_____ 37. Although she's a chef, she seems unwilling to teach (it   cooking) to me.
                                                                 A   B

_____38. I bought three items (<u>:</u> <u>;</u>) a book, a pen, and staples.
                                                                   C D

_____39. My grief abated, and I could cry no (<u>farther</u>   <u>further</u>).
                                                                                 F   G

_____40. The cost of an apartment in San Francisco has (<u>raised</u>   <u>risen</u>) a great deal in the past decade.
                                                                                                   A   B

_____41. I like Boston more than (<u>any</u>   <u>any other</u>) city in the United States..
                                                                         C   D

_____42. Twain's writing style is less bawdy than (<u>Shakespeare</u>   <u>Shakespeare's</u>).
                                                                             F   G

_____43. Boston is much more livable than (<u>any</u>   <u>any other</u>) city on the West Coast.
                                                                      A   B

_____44. After quitting for a year the woman (<u>again reverted</u>   <u>went back</u>) to a pack per day habit
                                                                          C   D

_____45. <u>A Dutch boy took his finger from a dike, leading a city to flood.</u>
                       F
              <u>When a Dutch boy removed his finger from a dyke, a city flooded.</u>
                       G

_____46. Appreciating the performance, (<u>no applause was spared by the audience</u>
                                                                               A
              <u>the audience spared no applause</u>).
                   B

_____47. The Cuban missile crisis occurred in the (<u>1960's</u>   <u>1960s</u>).
                                                                C   D

_____48. Grandma gave my brother more love than (<u>I</u>   <u>me</u>).
                                                               F   G

_____49. For breakfast the chef prepared grapefruit, toast, (<u>bacon,</u>   <u>bacon</u>) and eggs.
                                                                                A   B

_____50. The highwaymen were (<u>laying</u>   <u>lying</u>) in wait for unsuspecting travelers.
                                                                   C   D

Two-Way Choice III 51-75

case	(*nominative, possessive, objective*)	**p**	punctuation
c̲	capitalization	**pref**	pronoun agreement/reference error
comp	improper comparison	**ros**	run-on sentence, comma splice
d	diction, wrong word, part of speech	**sp**	spelling
frag	fragment; not a sentence	**s/v**	subject ≠ verb agreement
mm	misplaced or faulty modifier	**sub**	upside down ↔ subordination
nn	double negative	**t**	tense
#	number (*singular / plural*)	**ww**	wordy, repetitive, tautological
¶	paragraph		
//	parallel structure	**√**	correct, ok

_____ 51. The toddler leapt (<u>in</u> <u>into</u>) the muddy pond, causing a muddy splash.
　　　　　　　　　　　　　　　　A   B

_____ 52. My sister is reluctant to do (<u>spring</u> <u>Spring</u>) cleaning.
　　　　　　　　　　　　　　　　　　　　D   F

_____ 53. What the matron enjoyed was her dear (<u>friends</u> <u>friends'</u>) visiting her.
　　　　　　　　　　　　　　　　　　　　　　　　　A   B

_____ 54. Between you and (<u>I</u> <u>me</u>) lies a vast age difference.
　　　　　　　　　　　　　　　　　　D   F

_____ 55. The wannabe recruit had been (<u>lieing</u> <u>lying</u>) about his age.
　　　　　　　　　　　　　　　　　　　　　　　A   B

_____ 56. Neither the shorter guys nor I (<u>am</u> <u>are</u>) ready to play basketball.
　　　　　　　　　　　　　　　　　　　　　　C   D

_____ 57. A well-planned experiment is one (<u>where</u> <u>in which</u>) there is a control.
　　　　　　　　　　　　　　　　　　　　　　A   B

_____ 58. Her chores (<u>having been</u> <u>being</u>) done, the girl decides to nap
　　　　　　　　　　　　　　　　C   D

_____ 59. None of my classmates is stronger than (<u>me</u> <u>I</u>) when it comes to lifts.
　　　　　　　　　　　　　　　　　　　　　　　　A   B

_____ 60. She was not only a beauty queen but a superb athlete (<u>as well</u>   <u>as well in</u>
<u>addition</u>).　　　　　　　　　　　　　　　　　　　　　　　C   D

_____ 61. The novice was fascinated with undersea (<u>phenomena</u> <u>phenomenon</u>).
　　　　　　　　　　　　　　　　　　　　　　　F   G

_____ 62. After two hours, the majority of the crew (want wants) to quit.
                                                      A   B

_____ 63. This book of poetry is better than (any any other) non-fiction work.
                                                  C   D

_____ 64. I read the Herman Melville (novel, novel) *Moby Dick*.
                                          F   G

_____ 65. Both Mary and her sister by age 25 had become (a doctor doctors).
                                                             A   B

_____ 66. Since the Civil War the United States (has have) been a sovereign nation.
                                                     C   D

_____ 67. Winston tastes good (as like) a cigarette should.
                                   F   G

_____ 68. The History 101 course (curriculum curricula) proved challenging.
                                      A   B

_____ 69. I needed relief so (bad badly) that I took three aspirin.
                                  C   D

_____ 70. The coach told (we us) boys to shape up or be cut from the team.
                              F   G

_____ 71. Diet soda has 70% (fewer less) calories than the regular kind of cola.
                                 A   B

_____ 72. Unlike most people, I'm not (adverse averse) to eating turnips.
                                           C   D

_____ 73. The troubled youth sought (council counsel) from a dean.
                                         F   G

_____ 74. The teen hopes to (graduate graduate from) high school in 2018.
                                 A   B

_____ 75. A good group photo is one (where in which) everyone's smiling at once.
                                         C   D

Two-Way Choice IV 76-100

case	(*nominative, possessive, objective*)	**p**	punctuation
c	capitalization	**pref**	pronoun agreement/reference error
comp	improper comparison	**ros**	run-on sentence, comma splice
d	diction, wrong word, part of speech	**sp**	spelling
frag	fragment; not a sentence	**s/v**	subject ≠ verb agreement
mm	misplaced or faulty modifier	**sub**	upside down ↔ subordination
nn	double negative	**t**	tense
#	number (*singular / plural*)	**ww**	wordy, repetitive, tautological
¶	paragraph		
//	parallel structure	**√**	correct, ok

_____ 76. I too don't feel terribly (<u>good</u>   <u>well</u>) when you are unhappy.
                                                                                                                  F   G

_____ 77. From his wrinkled brow I (<u>inferred</u>   <u>implied</u>) his displeasure.
                                                                                      A   B

_____ 78. The enmity between the pair was evident by (<u>their</u>   <u>them</u>) sitting apart.
                                                                                                                C   D

_____ 79. The mad dictator had (<u>illusions</u>   <u>delusions</u>) of world domination.
                                                                                   F   G

_____ 80. After a heavy lunch I (<u>lay</u>   <u>laid</u>   <u>lied</u>) down for a nap.
                                                                             A   B   C

_____ 81. I'm not going to attend, and the reason is (<u>that</u>   <u>because</u>) I feel ill.
                                                                                                       D   F

_____ 82. What is the (<u>affect</u>   <u>effect</u>) of gamma rays on marigold plants?
                                                             A   B

_____ 83. Having lost a cat myself, I felt (<u>empathy</u>   <u>sympathy</u>) for the boy whose
                            Siamese was run over.   A   B

_____ 84. Decisions on the bequest were made by the (<u>principal</u>   <u>principle</u>) heirs.
                                                                                            F   G

_____ 85. My orthodontist's (<u>avocation</u>   <u>vocation</u>) is dentistry.
                                                 A   B

_____ 86. The song was titled: (<u>"My Only Sunshine".</u>   <u>"My Only Sunshine."</u>)
                                                                       B   C

_____87. The weather is uncertain, (which   a situation which) frustrates my plans.
                                          D   F

_____88. My (co-worker's   co-worker) repeatedly coming in late annoys our boss.
                     A   B

_____89. He couldn't decide (among   between) an unexpected surplus of job offers.
                                    C   D

_____90. After a strenuous workout I like to jump (in   into) the shower.
                                                        F   G

_____91. At summer camp I rarely do (like   as) I'm told by the junior staff.
                                           A   B

_____92. Nobody feels worse about the fire damage than (I   me).
                                                              C   D

_____93. (We   Us) fraternity boys need to stick together.
                F   G

_____94. The man and his dog (likes   like) to go on long walks.
                                     A   B

_____95. The doctor's not in his office today, I don't suppose.
                          C   D

_____96. The bride along with her husband (is   are) getting in the car.
                                                 F   G

_____97. I wish he'd return whence he came from.
                                   A   B

_____98. If I (had   had had) the money I would've bought the iPhone today.
                     C   D

_____99. For the pirate drama the actor used a cane and (affected   effected) a limp.
                                                                F   G

_____100. (Though   While) he disliked long trips, he nevertheless joined our caravan.
                  A   B

Answers

I 1-25	II 26-50	III 51-75
1. A t	26. D mm	51. B d
2. D //	27. F t	52. D c
3. B d	28. B #	53. B case
4. C nn	29. D mm	54. F case
5. B t	30. G mm	55. B sp
6. D d	31. B case	56. C s/v
7. B case	32. D d	57. B pref
8. D nn	33. F case	58. D t
9. B case	34. B sub	59. B case
10. D d	35. D d	60. C ww
11. F pref	36. B s/v	61. F #
12. B d	37. B pref	62. B s/v
13. G s/v	38. C p	63. C comp
14. B s/v	39. G d	64. G p
15. C sp	40. A d	65. B #
16. A d	41. D comp	66. C s/v
17. C case	42. G case	67. F comp
18. F ww	43. A comp	68. A #
19. B s/v	44. D d	69. C d
20. D s/v	45. G mm	70. G case
21. G mm	46. B mm	71. A d
22. A nn	47. D p	72. D d
23. D d	48. G case	73. G d
24. G t	49. B d	74. B d
25. B t	50. D d	75. D pref

IV

76-100

76. F d
77. A d
78. C case
79. G d
80. A d
81. D nn
82. B d
83. A d
84. F d
85. B d
86. B p
87. F pref
88. A case
89. C d
90. G d
91. B d
92. C case
93. F case
94. B s/v
95. D nn
96. F s/v
97. A ww
98. D t
99. F d
100. A d

Abusage

Presented here is a continuation of mixed, brief, and self-pacing practices exemplifying violations in the conventions of proper formal grammar and syntax.

Abusage I   1-15

In the blank put the corresponding correction symbol.

case	(*nominative, possessive, objective*)	**p**	punctuation
c	capitalization	**pref**	pronoun agreement/reference error
comp	improper comparison	**ros**	run-on sentence, comma splice
d	diction, wrong word, part of speech	**sp**	spelling
frag	fragment; not a sentence	**s/v**	subject ≠ verb agreement
mm	misplaced or faulty modifier	**sub**	upside down ↔ subordination
nn	double negative	**t**	tense
#	number (*singular / plural*)	**ww**	wordy, repetitive, tautological
¶	paragraph		
//	parallel structure	**√**	correct, ok

1. _____ In the 1960's hippies and flower children comprised a colorful subculture.

2. _____ I can think of some excuses but none seems plausible.

3. _____ By dusk we had enough of practice, and, exhausted, we had gone inside.

4. _____ He's ungrateful. Wasn't it us who helped him when he was in trouble?

5. _____ The movie, ending with the demise of the hero, made even me kind of sad.

6. _____ As to whose husband were a better cook, both sisters-in-law were agreed.

7. _____ Although they decided to take a walk, the wind was blowing a fierce gale.

8. _____ The number of Florida vacationers unquestionably have increased each year.

9. _____ Only one of the boys who try out will be team captain.

10. _____ I was very dissapointed when I found out my score on the quiz.

11. _____ Despite the scientific statistics gathering, the data collected was useless.

12. _____ The candidate believed the media were responsible for him losing the election.

13. _____ I'd cancel the trip, if the decision was up to me.

14. _____ After a strenuous workout, who wouldn't want to jump in the shower?

15. _____ I hoped my grandma would loan me money for college tuition this fall.

Abusage II 16-30

case	(*nominative, possessive, objective*)	**p**	punctuation
c	capitalization	**pref**	pronoun agreement/reference error
comp	improper comparison	**ros**	run-on sentence, comma splice
d	diction, wrong word, part of speech	**sp**	spelling
frag	fragment; not a sentence	**s/v**	subject ≠ verb agreement
mm	misplaced or faulty modifier	**sub**	upside down ↔ subordination
nn	double negative	**t**	tense
#	number (*singular / plural*)	**ww**	wordy, repetitive, tautological
¶	paragraph		
//	parallel structure	**√**	correct, ok

16. _____ I received a BA degree when I graduated college early in June.

17. _____ Obsessed with no other woman's charms, Romeo couldn't help but think of Juliet.

18. _____ An unpopular girl is willing to go to the prom with whomever asks her.

19. _____ My brother blasting the TV kept me from concentrating on important work.

20. _____ It was made clear that us boys were unwelcome to attend.

21. _____ Should you need me, don't hesitate to stop by irregardless of the hour.

22. _____ The struts in the radar tower are deployed in quite a unique configuration.

23. _____ We planned to arrive on time, to paint the porch, to mow the lawn, and lastly water the garden.

24. _____ The voters in Massachusetts are as a rule more liberal than in Vermont.

25. _____ The three blind mice had no sense of direction between them.

26. _____ We told the usher that we only could stay until intermission.

27. _____ Just those people with cars living in the condos may park there.

28. _____ People, who live in glass houses, shouldn't throw stones.

29. _____ We located the meeting place he mentioned without difficulty.

30. _____ Measles is bad, however, mumps are worse.

Abusage III 31-45

case	(*nominative, possessive, objective*)	**p**	punctuation
c	capitalization	**pref**	pronoun agreement/reference error
comp	improper comparison	**ros**	run-on sentence, comma splice
d	diction, wrong word, part of speech	**sp**	spelling
frag	fragment; not a sentence	**s/v**	subject ≠ verb agreement
mm	misplaced or faulty modifier	**sub**	upside down ↔ subordination
nn	double negative	**t**	tense
#	number (*singular / plural*)	**ww**	wordy, repetitive, tautological
¶	paragraph		
//	parallel structure	**√**	correct, ok

31. _____ When touring Boston for the first time, the Freedom Trail is a must-do.

32. _____ We enjoy bargain clothing made in Asia, although the imports direly threaten U.S. jobs and our trade balance.

33. _____ The coach told the injured player to shed his gear and lay down on the bench.

34. _____ Neither the members of the orchestra nor the conductor have music stands.

35. _____ They couldn't help but laugh at the outrageous political satire.

36. _____ You're saying that you graduated college the same year as I?

37. _____ A soloist together with members of a chorus are performing in Boston tonight.

38. _____ To me as a ten year old boy, *National Geographic* photos of topless tribeswomen were racy.

39. _____ Our next door neighbors, the Jones', are moving within a month.

40. _____ Knowing they'd try blaming us, I said neither I nor my siblings was responsible.

41. _____ Entrance to the roller coaster ride was based solely on the criteria of height.

42. _____ "That was a close call!", she shrieked. "Please slow down."

43. _____ Tom, Dick, and Harry counted all of six dollars between them.

44. _____ If I had been laying down on the job, then how'd it get done on time?

45. _____ To the picnic we brought: all-beef hotdogs and German potato salad.

Abusage IV 46-60

case	(*nominative, possessive, objective*)	**p**	punctuation
c	capitalization	**pref**	pronoun agreement/reference error
comp	improper comparison	**ros**	run-on sentence, comma splice
d	diction, wrong word, part of speech	**sp**	spelling
frag	fragment; not a sentence	**s/v**	subject ≠ verb agreement
mm	misplaced or faulty modifier	**sub**	upside down ↔ subordination
nn	double negative	**t**	tense
#	number (*singular / plural*)	**ww**	wordy, repetitive, tautological
¶	paragraph		
//	parallel structure	**√**	correct, ok

46. _____ When the show was over, we didn't know what to think or who to thank.

47. _____ Statistics indicates that smokers don't live as long as non-smokers.

48. _____ While the door was open and there was welcome sign, we decided to go inside.

49. _____ Seeing the scowl on her face, we guests felt sort of unwanted.

50. _____ He wanted a medication; that prescribed by a doctor.

51. _____ Infants can be fun, but I sure avoid changing their diapers if at all possible.

52. _____ Whom do you want to invite beside me and my parents?

53. _____ It's an open question whether I were to be project leader.

54. _____ Excelling at a foreign language, several years' study will be required.

55. _____ The commander didn't doubt but that the raids would resume soon.

56. _____ My cousins live on the Southern shore of Long Island, New York.

57. _____ The Statue of Liberty loomed over we who were visiting Ellis Island.

58. _____ Fame and a crown awaited whomever withdrew the sword from the stone.

59. _____ He was tired and hungry and broke, and it made him feel miserable.

60. _____ His access to insider information resulted in the broker getting rich.

Answers

1. p
2. s/v
3. t
4. case
5. d
6. t
7. sub
8. s/v
9. s/v
10. sp
11. s/v
12. case
13. t
14. d
15. d

16. d
17. nn
18. case
19. case
20. case
21. d
22. d
23. //
24. comp
25. d
26. mm
27. mm
28. p
29. mm
30. s/v

31. mm
32. sub
33. d or t*
34. s/v
35. nn
36. d
37. s/v
38. p
39. case
40. s/v
41. #
42. p
43. d
44. d
45. p

46. case
47. s/v
48. d
49. d
50. p
51. d
52. d
53. t
54. mm
55. nn
56. <u>c</u>
57. case
58. case
59. pref
60. case

*Lay in the present tense means to put down. Lay is also the past tense of lie, which means to assume rest in a horizontal position.

Proficiency

The two score additional practice quizzes here apply to formal written, as opposed to conversational, English. The errors are deliberately mixed — although in the interest of economy, there are no examples of paragraphing ¶ problems.

Proficiency I   1–20

Insert the proper correction symbol in the blank.

1. _____ If he hadn't concealed his grin so well, I might of known that he was up to mischief.

2. _____ My brother Jonathan is quite different than the rest of our siblings.

3. _____ Had we ever been able to unlock it, the treasure would have been a most unique find.

4. _____ By the end of the day, John was considerably farther along in the assignment than Steven.

5. _____ After escaping from the crate, the nearby forest became the dog's refuge.

6. _____ I won't do my homework, regardless of the effect that it will have on my grade.

7. _____ The football star proudly flouted his sports scholarship to his teammates.

8. _____ The jungle climate and humidity proved adverse to our planned hike.

9. _____ I thought I would do well on the exam, but the result left me kind of disappointed.

10. _____ The cop ordered the suspects to surrender their weapons and lay down on the ground.

11. _____ I didn't have enough cash to afford dinner, but my brother was able to loan me a few dollars.

12. _____ The reason for his tardiness was because his work meeting ran later than usual.

13. _____ My mother had on high heels when she tripped and got stuck in a sewer grating.

14. _____ Will anyone else be attending the lecture beside me?

15. _____ She was never on time, and that bothered me no end.

16. _____ I remained a friendly, but disinterested mediator in their family feud.

17. _____ My brother winning the award was a remarkable achievement, one that I was proud of.

18. _____ The party chairman thinks the media has been unfair to his candidate.

19. _____ Neither the neighbors nor he were aware of the local burglary.

20. _____ His proficiency at the piano was due to the amount of hours he spent practicing.

Proficiency II 21-40

Insert the proper correction symbol in the blank.

21. _____ The heat of the desert made it a tortuous journey for all but the most experienced hiker.

22. _____ A carpenter typically clamps his fine woodwork in a vice.

23. _____ A new suspension in the car insured a smooth ride.

24. _____ When just a toddler, the medical profession began to appeal to the boy.

25. _____ Among us three, we had just enough tokens to earn the prize from the arcade.

26. _____ A repetitive learner makes the same mistakes over and over again.

27. _____ No one in the house likes cooking accept me.

28. _____ You need to allot money for monthly membership to the new country club.

29. _____ You can see a shimmering blue if you look in my eyes.

30. _____ I didn't feel too good after riding the new roller coaster at the amusement park.

31. _____ You shouldn't feel bad as long as you gave the assignment your best shot.

32. _____ At the end of the story, the wolf drowned after being stuffed with stones.

33. _____ Caesar said, "The die is cast" as he defied the Senate's order to abandon his legions.

34. _____ The continuous arguments next door kept me awake.

35. _____ By burning the crops in their retreat, any food supply was denied to the advancing army.

36. _____ Shall I carry your coat for you or can you manage by yourself?

37. _____ The motorist didn't notice the imminent danger of the car wreck in front of him.

38. _____ Has Mary graduated college already?

39. _____ I was in no way certain that snow will fall before the weekend.

40. _____ Loyalty to the partners was the major criteria for advancement in the law firm.

Proficiency III 41-60
Insert the proper correction symbol in the blank.

41. _____ The city of Harrisburg is the capitol of Pennsylvania.

42. _____ A nickel has a worth of fewer pennies than a dime.

43. _____ No amount of apologies will make up for the betrayal that I currently feel.

44. _____ Coming to agreement is tough if one party was averse to compromising.

45. _____ Hallucinogenic drugs taken under adverse conditions can create delusions of prosecution.

46. _____ The landlord had no problem filling the his condo units with tenets.

47. _____ He always woke up extra early in the morning to assure that he would make it to class on time.

48. _____ In the olden days, criminals were hung in the town square for the whole population to witness.

49. _____ If you don't focus, you may never finish before the deadline, I don't believe.

50. _____ The graph was helpful to me, as the data were very confusing.

51. _____ I have never met anyone from the South until I went to Texas on vacation.

52. _____ The boat was enormous and her canvas sails were gloriously unfurled.

53. _____ You should of never allowed a perfect stranger into your house.

54. _____ She cooked dinner in a ceramic crock pot, which was a new treat for us.

55. _____ When I challenged Tim to a race together, I told him that the best man would win.

56. _____ The man in the alley I knew to be he, a 60 year-old onetime broker, now turned beggar.

57. _____ This was he, the man we chose for the privelege of being our senator.

58. _____ Jack never leaves his house before brushing his teeth and he puts his shoes on.

59. _____ The vegetable soup contained carrots, leeks, potatoes, parsley, et alia.

60. _____ Armed with deadly weapons, the duel matched expert swordsmen.

Proficiency IV 61-80

Insert the proper correction symbol in the blank.

61. _____ The thief turned out to be the one among us who we respected most.

62. _____ The increase in luxury car sales have exceeded everyone's expectations.

63. _____ The older one grows, the more you regret not taking more opportunities in your youth.

64. _____ Everyone had their own reasons for voting as they did.

65. _____ In their common meetings together, the entire group worked with one another as a whole.

66. _____ To arrive on time to class daily, an early schedule must be maintained.

67. _____ I can't help but suspect that he is up to no good.

68. _____ With no dissenting vote never heard at all, the bill was quickly passed.

69. _____ The cars honked their horns in celebration continually, and it kept me awake well past midnight.

70. _____ We'll get on the road tomorrow at dawn, irrespective of the weather.

71. _____ In the summer shore I liked sunbathing, playing beach ball, and then just to float on the waves.

72. _____ I am very strong in English and History, but I was never good at other subjects.

73. _____ Although my cousin is a chemistry teacher, he doesn't want to teach it to me.

74. _____ I can't unscrew the cover on this jar. Can you do it for me?

75. _____ John who is my best friend is very enthusiastic and outgoing.

76. _____ Dickens' novel, *A Tale of Two Cities*, is a staple in English literature.

77. _____ We looked everywhere for the missing necklace, it was nowhere to be seen.

78. _____ I see no reason to pay for your education; since you haven't been putting in any effort.

79. _____ My brother enjoys baseball, my sister plays volleyball.

80. _____ Peter showed us the medal he won with great pride at the fencing tournament.

Proficiency V   81-100

Insert the proper correction symbol in the blank.

81. _____ I just saw a movie featuring dancing ballerinas on the television.

82. _____ I was taught that it is impolite not to gracefully except a gift.

83. _____ The principal reason for her angry disposition stems from childhood abuse.

84. _____ Occasionally we could hear yelling now and then from the haunted woods.

85. _____ In my view you should wear the blue dress as it complements your eyes, I think.

86. _____ Although he lost a considerable amount of weight, he was still heavier than anybody in the gym.

87. _____ Scrooge is a bigger miser than any person in the world.

88. _____ Closing the door, she walked in her office and began to fill out forms.

89. _____ Have you or has either one of you two finished your chores?

90. _____ She likes to jog for a while, then cool off, and then to sprint the last 100 yards.

91. _____ The book will surely be successful due to its insightful commentary and because it's humorous.

92. _____ Da Vinci is not only famous for his artwork but also his inventions.

93. _____ Yesterday I had put the laundry in the dryer, and this morning it is dried.

94. _____ I am the first to admit he can be manipulative, passive aggressive, and that he has a mean streak.

95. _____ Although I gave two weeks' notice, my boss still disapproved of me not telling him sooner.

96. _____ The perpetrator is him, the man currently behind the stand.

97. _____ If the sun was over the horizon, then it was time for my departure.

98. _____ I couldn't have possibly taken the money, so it must of been someone else.

99. _____ Who else is going to wear a costume beside me?

100. _____ Who else is to be blamed except my brother and I?

Proficiency VI 101-120

Insert the proper correction symbol in the blank.

101. _____ All but Jonathan and us were involved in the masquerade.

102. _____ The blues singer with his Dixieland band were headlining the show.

103. _____ Mary's wide expertise in math, science, and literature allow her to ace exams.

104. _____ There seem to be several conflicts in my work schedule.

105. _____ Each one of the candidates are required to complete an interview and physical examination.

106. _____ Neither my mother nor I am able to answer your question.

107. _____ The school board are ready to release their nomination for the new principal.

108. _____ The sole criteria for admission were a warm body and a willing mind.

109. _____ Everyone in the bleachers is hoping that their favored team will win the game.

110. _____ Each one of you students must bring your own signed permission slip to go to the zoo.

111. _____ In a gold envelope, his birthday wish for concert tickets had been granted.

112. _____ Sitting in the lodge, I watched the skier win the race.

113. _____ To donate blood, two hours must be set aside.

114. _____ On entering the museum, a hall of portraits from the 1800s came into view.

115. _____ When only one week old, my parents brought my new sister home from the hospital.

116. _____ From the far side of the house, Sam and I could hear hardly a word of the heated argument.

117. _____ Although you didn't finish, there can't be any doubt that you tried.

118. _____ As we walked through the eerie darkness, I couldn't help sensing danger.

119. _____ Do you imagine she's going to be angry for us not waiting for her?

120. _____ What sort of surprise did you have in mind for the children?

Proficiency VII 121-140

Insert the proper correction symbol in the blank.

121. _____ I emailed her many times last week, but I never have received even a short reply.

122. _____ I found my laptop in the library exactly where I left it the day prior.

123. _____ I would have liked to meet with you last week regarding our joint project.

124. _____ The cop informed me that he couldn't refrain from writing a ticket even if he wants to.

125. _____ Many ancient scientists believed that the earth was flat.

126. _____ If I was afraid, I didn't show it and thereby alarm my compatriots.

127. _____ If I'd studied a little more often last semester, my GPA would be much higher.

128. _____ To catch our connecting flight: We will have to hope for no further delays.

129. _____ When out of immediate danger, a big sense of relief came over me.

130. _____ Running to catch the bus, I slipped on the ice and broke my arm.

131. _____ Mary is routinely moody, which damages her relationships with friends.

132. _____ Although I know all of the answers, I have refused to divulge them.

133. _____ Before she came home John's mother reminded the boy to complete his chores.

134. _____ My twin brother George is an excellent swimmer and a passable diver.

135. _____ Tripping on the curb, my briefcase's contents spilled onto the sidewalk.

136. _____ That is the doddering old professor, who just walked past us.

137. _____ *Mary Had a Little Lamb* is a rhyme familiar to any toddler.

138. _____ The map showed we needed to head Northwest to find the meeting place.

139. _____ Jim chose partying instead of finishing assignments, consequently he will not graduate.

140. _____ I only do work in the office, nowhere else.

Proficiency VIII 141-160

Insert the proper correction symbol in the blank.

141. _____ My brother sold me the textbook on his desk, which he had used previously.

142. _____ An avid fan of movies, no new releases were passed up by John as soon as they came out.

143. _____ We just heard about a local factory's explosion on the radio.

144. _____ Called the "city that never sleeps", New York is busier than any other city in the U.S.

145. _____ My score on the exam was higher than my less academically gifted brother.

146. _____ Laying down on my bed, I was so comfortable that I didn't want to turn the lights off.

147. _____ Climbing Mt. Everest is a torturous endeavor, one that many people don't walk out of alive.

148. _____ The annual town census excepted those who were only temporary residents.

149. _____ Everyone was requested to contribute to the fund drive as much as they could afford.

150. _____ The mosquito made a continuous buzzing noise as it flew around the room.

151. _____ Although I was worried about him, I knew that he wasn't in eminent danger.

152. _____ I can ensure you that I will be home safely before midnight.

153. _____ Many important legislative decisions have been made in the capital building.

154. _____ Honor, integrity, and compassion are a few vital tenants in my life.

155. _____ The foreigner man balked at undressing for a physical, being done by a female physician.

156. _____ The amount of men injured in the war was staggeringly high.

157. _____ I wouldn't have done so bad on the test if I had read up on the subject.

158. _____ In comparative musical talents, she was by far the twin most talented.

159. _____ Hemingway was one of the best short story writers who I've ever read.

160. _____ The reason for his reluctance to join us was that the prices seemed excessive.

Proficiency IX   161-180

Insert the proper correction symbol in the blank.

161. _____ Nobody likes it when they are subjected to ridicule.

162. _____ Every single, solitary soul was expected to do his individual duty.

163. _____ Who, beside Hannah and me, is eligible to participate in the bridge tournament.

164. _____ He scaled Mt. Washington which is in New Hampshire.

165. _____ While not yet house broken, I let the puppy loose in the house.

166. _____ Hoping to hear from you soon, next time please call before midnight.

167. _____ Have either of you guys completed the town survey yet?

168. _____ This summer my birthday falls on a Thursday; when I'll be away at camp.

169. _____ On the radio we heard about the armed robbery's occurring at our kitchen table.

170. _____ The author, whose works I enjoy the most, is Edgar Allen Poe.

171. _____ In my opinion, I think she's lost control of her senses when she acts so irrationally.

172. _____ While she was born without a father, she was shy around men.

173. _____ If I was working, I didn't want to be disturbed.

174. _____ You are completely and utterly wrong in your mistaken assertions.

175. _____ She was elegant, beautiful, and knew how to dress well.

176. _____ My maternal grandmother who was raised in Italy struggles to adopt American customs.

177. _____ After our last performance, I worry that the teacher had too high expectations of us.

178. _____ After the man was told of his blunder, he apologized without hardly any hesitation.

179. _____ I only told the secret to one other person.

180. _____ Give the extra tickets to whomever you think would enjoy them the most.

Proficiency X   191-200

Insert the proper correction symbol in the blank.

181. _____ Everyone was surprised at the teenager setting a state record in the 800 meter sprint.

182. _____ My brother sneered and turned up the volume just to aggravate me.

183. _____ I must admit that I am not a passionate wrestler, but my brother is obsessed with it.

184. _____ My older brother seems like a better version of myself.

185. _____ It appears to be he who is stealing the cookies from the kitchen.

186. _____ After the interruption, we all returned back to work.

187. _____ I was determined to win the contest, irregardless of how.

188. _____ Greenhouse gasses are said to effect a hotter climate.

189. _____ His anger was due largely to his sister taking his belongings without asking.

190. _____ My yawn most assuredly signaled my disinterest in the topic of discussion.

191. _____ Although we started work at the same time, soon I had progressed considerably further.

192. _____ I enjoy Mahler's symphonies much more than Tchaikovsky.

193. _____ Just who are you trying to impress?

194. _____ Neither James nor his fellow classmates have completed their reports as instructed.

195. _____ My aunt, who became a widow early, can sure sympathize with other bereaved women.

196. _____ If you listened carefully to the instructions, you wouldn't have made such a careless error.

197. _____ The clerk repeatedly mispronounced our names, which began to irritate me.

198. _____ The newly compiled data shows that fewer crimes are being committed now.

199. _____ To improve his chances, several more lottery tickets were bought.

200. _____ Las Vegas has more divorces per capita than any city in the West.

Answers

Proficiency I	Proficiency II	Proficiency III
1. d	21. d	41. d
2. comp	22. d	42. √
3. d	23. d	43. d
4. d	24. mm	44. t
5. mm	25. √	45. √
6. √	26. ww	46. d
7. d	27. d	47. d
8. √	28. √	48. d
9. d	29. d	49. nn
10. d	30. d	50. √
11. d	31. √	51. t
12. nn	32. t	52. p
13. sub	33. √	53. d
14. d	34. d	54. pref
15. pref	35. mm	55. d
16. √	36. √	56. case
17. case	37. √	57. sp
18. s/v	38. d	58. //
19. s/v	39. t	59. d
20. d	40. #	60. mm

Proficiency IV	Proficiency V	Proficiency VI
61. case	81. mm	101 case
62. s/v	82. d	102 s/v
63. d	83. d	103 s/v
64. pref	84. ww	104 √
65. ww	85. ww	105 s/v
66. mm	86. t	106 √
67. nn	87. comp	107 s/v
68. nn	88. d	108 √
69. pref	89. √	109 pref
70. √	90. //	110 √
71. //	91. //	111 mm
72. c	92. comp	112 √
73. pref	93. t	113 mm
74. pref	94. //	114 mm
75. p	95. case	115 mm
76. p	96. case	116 √
77. ros	97. √	117 √
78. p	98. d	118 √
79. ros	99. d	119 case
80. mm	100 case	120. √

Proficiency VII	Proficiency VIII	Proficiency IX
121. t	141. mm	161 pref
122. t	142. mm	162 ww
123. √	143. mm	163 d
124. t	144. √	164 p
125. t	145. case	165 mm
126. t	146. d	166 mm
127. √	147. √	167 s/v
128. p	148. √	168 p
129. mm	149. pref	169 mm
130. √	150. √	170 p
131. pref	151. d	171 ww
132. √	152. d	172 d
133. mm	153. d	173 √
134. p	154. d	174 ww
135. mm	155. √	175 //
136. √	156. d	176 p
137. p	157. d	177 t
138. c	158. comp	178 nn
139. ros	159. case	179 mm
140. mm	160 √	180 case

Proficiency X

181 case

182 d

183 pref

184 √

185 case

186 ww

187 d

188 √

189 case

190 d

191 √

192 case or comp

193 case

194 √

195 d

196 t

197 pref

198 s/v

199 mm

200 comp

Mastery

Extended review exercises.

Mastery I   1-25

case	(*nominative, possessive, objective*)	**p**	punctuation
c̲	capitalization	**pref**	pronoun agreement/reference error
comp	improper comparison	**ros**	run-on sentence, comma splice
d	diction, wrong word, part of speech	**sp**	spelling
frag	fragment; not a sentence	**s/v**	subject ≠ verb agreement
mm	misplaced or faulty modifier	**sub**	upside down ↔ subordination
nn	double negative	**t**	tense
#	number (*singular / plural*)	**ww**	wordy, repetitive, tautological
¶	paragraph		
//	parallel structure	**√**	correct, ok

_____ 1. I enjoy not only the short stories of Edgar Allen Poe but Hemingway as well.

_____ 2. I wish I could be learning Chinese, eating Chinese food, and travel to China.

_____ 3. Sometimes I feel that my mother has expectations that are too high of my brother and I, but I try my best to live up to those expectations.

_____ 4. As I entered the classroom as school was ending, I unfortunately discovered that the teacher whom I was seeking no longer works there.

_____ 5. It is said that there is no such thing as a bad question, but there certainly seems to be plenty.

_____ 6. In my opinion, Beethoven was one of the best composers who has ever written symphonies.

_____ 7. Everyone in the class was encouraged to work as hard as they could on the final project, which was worth a large portion of their grade.

_____ 8. Every student is expected to do homework each night, however, some nights I'm just too tired to do work.

_____ 9. When a hairy, black spider dropped on her desk and ran up her sleeve, it caused her fear.

_____ 10. When only a teenager, programming enticed me more than any other hobby.

_____ 11. Did you know, without a penny scarcely saved up, I hitch-hiked across two states?

_____ 12. There can be no doubt, the sportscaster said, but that the Red Sox would win the game.

_____ 13. I wasn't sure that I should make it to my appointment on time, but I tried regardless.

_____ 14. Did he finish that difficult project altogether?

_____ 15. Since I could barely keep my eyes open, because I had not slept at all the previous night due to the sounds of construction outside my window.

_____ 16. While basketball is a fast paced sport: I enjoy soccer much more because of the agility required.

_____ 17. As soon as you have finished your analysis of our finances, please bring them to the conference room on the second floor.

_____ 18. Because of increased rainfall, my garden overflowed, and it caused the plants to die.

_____ 19. Homer's epic, *The Iliad,* preceded his *Odyssey* poem, the tale of Odysseus and his adventurous trials in returning to his homeland.

_____ 20. My brother lives in the South, loves being in the sun, but cannot stand the Northeast's Winter.

_____ 21. While my dog is an ugly cur, he didn't even place in the dog show.

_____ 22. Math has always been difficult for me, I struggle with even basic calculus as I am not able to understand even the fundamentals.

_____ 23. When she was so belated, it seemed like an eternity.

_____ 24. We heard about the horrendous turnpike traffic, and decided to take a more tortuous route.

_____ 25. At the end of the marathon, I doubt I could walk a step farther, but my brother seemed ready to run again.

Mastery II 26-50

case	(*nominative, possessive, objective*)	p	punctuation
c̲	capitalization	pref	pronoun agreement/reference error
comp	improper comparison	ros	run-on sentence, comma splice
d	diction, wrong word, part of speech	sp	spelling
frag	fragment; not a sentence	s/v	subject ≠ verb agreement
mm	misplaced or faulty modifier	sub	upside down ↔ subordination
nn	double negative	t	tense
#	number (*singular / plural*)	ww	wordy, repetitive, tautological
¶	paragraph		
//	parallel structure	√	correct, ok

_____ 26. The affect of not disciplining your children properly at an early age is often irreversible, as shown by studies launched by prominent psychiatrists.

_____ 27. The German measles are an illness normally associated with childhood

_____ 28. Every single individual citizen has an obligation to vote in this upcoming election, or else he or she can't complain about the candidate that becomes president.

_____ 29. Although I enunciate better than him, I must admit his speech is a lot more eloquent than mine.

_____ 30. A European car is typically much more luxurious than an American.

_____ 31. One definition of a snafu is where you get stuck on minor details.

_____ 32. His undaunted friend Michael, who was an adventurous risk taker, courageously dared to to ascend the steep mountain.

_____ 33. On Christmas morning, a shiny, red bike under the tree greeted the ecstatic girl.

_____ 34. This book discusses life changes caused by winning the lottery—how it effects the winner and may not bring future happiness.

_____ 35. His principle reason for wanting to become club president was because he craved recognition.

_____ 36. The amount of funds available will determine the amount of third-world children we can help.

_____ 37. All students are suppose to show their identification before entering the dormitory as a means of keeping out people who shouldn't enter.

_____ 38. He was further along in his development than other boys' were.

_____ 39. I have quit my job, moved away from home, and am beginning a new life for myself.

_____ 40. She gave water to the runners in plastic cups as they sped down the hill towards the finish line.

_____ 41. The dome of the U.S. capitol was refurbished st a cost of $59 million.

_____ 42. Students who cheat on their homework often escape punishment, but that should not deter you from completing your assignments honestly.

_____ 43. Shortly after leaving school, the radio announced the cancellation, and we all went home to celebrate.

_____ 44. My good works meant me being awarded a scholarship by the church.

_____ 45. The teacher thought it was a clever excuse; one that she had never heard before.

_____ 46. All because the lead actor was stuck in traffic causing the show's delayed for an hour..

_____ 47. Being able to read Shakespeare has gotten progressively easier, where each play has an index that explains the archaic language.

_____ 48. There are lots of rules in English grammar, sometimes you don't even know that your sentence is incorrect.

_____ 49. Her brother's bullying younger students made her ashamed to be his sister.

_____ 50. If you were worried about the storm, you would have gone to greater lengths to make sure that the windows were closed and the doors were bolted shut.

Mastery III 51-75

case	(*nominative, possessive, objective*)	**p**	punctuation
c	capitalization	**pref**	pronoun agreement/reference error
comp	improper comparison	**ros**	run-on sentence, comma splice
d	diction, wrong word, part of speech	**sp**	spelling
frag	fragment; not a sentence	**s/v**	subject ≠ verb agreement
mm	misplaced or faulty modifier	**sub**	upside down ↔ subordination
nn	double negative	**t**	tense
#	number (*singular / plural*)	**ww**	wordy, repetitive, tautological
¶	paragraph		
//	parallel structure	**√**	correct, ok

_____ 51. Jonathan laid in bed for too long and slept through the exam.

_____ 52. Mike said the matinee began at noon, but it actually started two hours' later.

_____ 53. The *Mona Lisa*, a portrait painted by Da Vinci, depicted a woman with an enigmatic smile.

_____ 54. After Halloween comes the best sales on candy, as many stores have leftovers that they wish to get rid of.

_____ 55. The chef's specialty are chicken dishes, although he also grills an excellent swordfish.

_____ 56. Neither my little siblings nor I was given a popsicle at the after school event.

_____ 57. Running away from one's problems doesn't make them go away; in fact, it can make your life even worse.

_____ 58. The team was kind of disappointed at losing the second game in a row.

_____ 59. You would think that after two hours of being in the ocean one would be tired.

_____ 60. Rat poison is harmful to whomever consumes it, and that is why it should be placed on a shelf far out of a child's reach.

_____ 61. Everyone is wondering who the new garden club president will be, although I'm fairly certain that it will be a female.

_____ 62. Michael's friends discovered that it was him who had broken the curve for the exam, effectively lowering everyone else's grade.

_____ 63. Someone who wishes to focus on their health must cut down on junk food and be more conscious of what they eat throughout the day.

_____ 64. One of the best perks of working with this company is their generous vacation policy.

_____ 65. He is normally considerably better at tennis than me, but yesterday I beat him two out of three games.

_____ 66. My parents want me to study to become a doctor, but I'm not interested in it.

_____ 67. Who do you trust when everyone seems to lie?

_____ 68. The officers told the troops that they were ready to do battle.

_____ 69. Many discreet details must be taken into account when assembling an airplane.

_____ 70. The cake ingredients are relative simple to prepare and are quite inexpensive.

_____ 71. He still did excellent on the test although his preparation was lackluster at best.

_____ 72. Make sure the soles of your shoes aren't muddy, while the car is a rental, and I can't afford to get it cleaned.

_____ 73. Although he was studying every day, he had performed poorly on the exam.

_____ 74. The principal's eighth-grade daughter was prettier than any girl in school.

_____ 75. My bakery's cakes are as good as any other bakery, but its cookies are the best that I have ever tasted.

Mastery IV   75-100

case	(*nominative, possessive, objective*)	**p**	punctuation
c	capitalization	**pref**	pronoun agreement/reference error
comp	improper comparison	**ros**	run-on sentence, comma splice
d	diction, wrong word, part of speech	**sp**	spelling
frag	fragment; not a sentence	**s/v**	subject ≠ verb agreement
mm	misplaced or faulty modifier	**sub**	upside down ↔ subordination
nn	double negative	**t**	tense
#	number (*singular / plural*)	**ww**	wordy, repetitive, tautological
¶	paragraph		
//	parallel structure	**√**	correct, ok

_____ 76. Although I had known him almost my whole life, I could still not trust him.

_____ 77. Pecos Bill was mean as a rattlesnake and twice as ornery.

_____ 78. That's Boston, Massachusetts; a beautiful city with a rich and diverse history.

_____ 79. All students who are interested in attending college, must send in an application before the deadline has past.

_____ 80. Whenever you are working with strong acids, you must wear goggles to prevent the liquid accidentally splashing up into your eyes.

_____ 81. The club president changes every year; the treasurer can be elected indefinately.

_____ 82. The Rogers' family consisted of two parents and six children.

_____ 83. I love to read books by authors such as: Shakespeare, Salinger, and Twain.

_____ 84. My favorite subject is science but I especially enjoy the following disciplines: chemistry and biology.

_____ 85. California was wild in the days of the old west.

_____ 86. Bill Belichick is my favorite coach in the National Football league.

_____ 87. Although I love to travel, I have never visited anywhere in the Southern Hemisphere.

_____ 88. My favorite book by Mark Twain is <u>The Adventures of Tom Sawyer</u>, although I am also fond of <u>The Adventures of Huckleberry Finn</u>.

_____ 89. Zeus is the most powerful God in all of Greek Mythology.

_____ 90. *The Compleat Angler*, written in the 1600s, is still considered the fisherman's Bible.

_____ 91. When attending the theatre, the play's storylines fascinate me as much the acting.

_____ 92. On our global vacation next year, we plan on visiting China and Greece, and then to travel to Mexico.

_____ 93. As soon as the school bell had at long last rang, we knew that we were finally free for the day.

_____ 94. Shortly after he had placed the cake in the oven, he realized that he forgot to add the final ingredient.

_____ 95. My parents were incredibly surprised at John winning the mathematics award, as my brother was never a strong student in the subject.

_____ 96. By practicing test questions every day and because he regularly attended tutoring, Steven earned the highest grade on the midterm exam.

_____ 97. In my opinion that girl's looks are not good as a Hollywood starlet's but better than most.

_____ 98. We waited in the airport for over two hours, later we learned that our flight had been delayed due to inclement weather conditions.

_____ 99. My brother, Steven, who is an Olympic sprinter, runs faster than my other brother does.

_____ 100. I cannot attend the concert due to work, so I will give the tickets to whoever asks first.

Mastery V 101-125

case	(*nominative, possessive, objective*)	**p**	punctuation
c	capitalization	**pref**	pronoun agreement/reference error
comp	improper comparison	**ros**	run-on sentence, comma splice
d	diction, wrong word, part of speech	**sp**	spelling
frag	fragment; not a sentence	**s/v**	subject ≠ verb agreement
mm	misplaced or faulty modifier	**sub**	upside down ↔ subordination
nn	double negative	**t**	tense
#	number (*singular / plural*)	**ww**	wordy, repetitive, tautological
¶	paragraph		
//	parallel structure	**√**	correct, ok

_____ 101. Tomorrow's game which will be the last game of the World Series will be between the Boston Red Sox and the New York Yankees.

_____ 102. If I worked carefully on the problem set, I probably wouldn't have lost as many points due to careless errors.

_____ 103. Today's computer with its fast processor speed and multiple cores is barely comparable to the computers of the 90's.

_____ 104. I saw the student talking to the professor after the class had ended; he was wearing an expensive designer blazer.

_____ 105. The *Tyrannosaurus rex* was a massive creature, it stood over 40 feet tall and weighed about nine tons.

_____ 106. We arrived late to the party, on account of the large degree of traffic and because John's car ran out of gas.

_____ 107. Waiting for me in the lobby, I saw my prom date, we linked arms, and we left for the dance.

_____ 108. They have neither fully completed and never even come close to finishing the job

_____ 109. Steven is one of those people that never admit to being wrong.

_____ 110. John pulled in the fish with a pointed gaff; it was nearly two feet long.

_____ 111. My housekeeper said while listening to the radio she felt happy.

_____ 112. I admit that I am not a strong swimmer, as I have not had a lot of practice, but my brother loves it.

_____ 113. Approaching home plate, all eyes were on the batter.

_____ 114. I am sure that it was John, not him, who vandalized the bathroom on the second floor.

_____ 115. When Uncle John was babysitting his nephew, he fell on the stairs and hit his head against the wall.

_____ 116. We should talk over the matter with a doctor, who we know is an expert surgeon.

_____ 117. You can't be too careful when it's not certain what obstacles one may face.

_____ 118. If I was to be in charge of the playground, I'd let dogs run off leash.

_____ 119. I wanted to arrive early to the party, but we were delayed by my younger sister taking too long to find her costume.

_____ 120. Before planning a vacation, a considerate employee will always let their boss know of the upcoming absence.

_____ 121. Although we made efforts to catch him, he leapt in car and drove far away in the distance.

_____ 122. Although Jonathan is a talented instrumentalist, he doesn't want to make it his career.

_____ 123. If I was as tall and lanky as he, I wouldn't wear short, baggy pants.

_____ 124. We walked gingerly past the planks where the bridge cracked the day before.

_____ 125. There was little doubt in my mind but that my brother had taken my tennis racket.

Answers

Mastery I 1 – 25	Mastery II 26-50	Mastery III 51-75
1. comp	26. d	51. d
2. //	27. s/v	52. p
3. case	28. ww	53. t
4. case	29. case	54. s/v
5. s/v	30. comp	55. s/v
6. s/v	31. √	56. √
7. pref	32. ww	57. pref
8. ros	33. mm	58. d
9. sub	34. d	59. pref
10. mm	35. nn	60. case
11. nn	36. d	61. √
12. nn	37. d	62. case
13. d	38. case	63. pref
14. √	39. //	64. pref
15. frag	40. mm	65. case
16. p	41. c	66. pref
17. pref	42. pref	67. case
18. pref	43. mm	68. mm
19. p	44. case	69. d
20. c	45. p	70. d
21. d	46. frag	71. d
22. ros	47. ros	72. d
23. pref	48. pref	73. t
24. p	49. √	74. comp
25. t	50. t	75. comp

Mastery IV	Mastery V
76-100	101-126
76. √	101. p
77. comp	102. t
78. p	103. p
79. d	104. pref
80. case	105. ros
81. sp	106. //
82. case	107. mm
83. p	108. nn
84. √	109. s/v
85. c̲	110. pref
86. c̲	111. mm
87. √	112. pref
88. p	113. mm
89. c̲	114. case
90. c̲	115. pref
91. mm	116. case
92. //	117. pref
93. t	118. t
94. t	119. case
95. case	120. pref
96. //	121. d
97. comp	122. pref
98. ros	123. t
99. p	124. t
100. √	125. nn

Challenge

Each item contains five variations of a sentence labeled A – E, one of which is grammatically and syntactically the correct. The remaining items taken together contain at least <u>two</u> discrete errors.

(1) Identify by letter the sentence among the five variations which needs no correction and write its letter A – E of that selection in the left hand blank.

(2) In the right hand blank write the correction symbol for at least <u>one</u> additional error among the remaining four variations.

Challenge 1-25

*Each set of five variations contains **at least two discrete errors**. Identify the sentence with **no error** by letter in the left hand blank, and beside it write the symbol for **one error** found in the four other choices. For an extra challenge you may find two errors.*
*Please bear in mind that an error involving an apostrophe could fall under case or p.

Correction symbols

case	(*nominative, possessive, objective*)	**p**	punctuation
c	capitalization	**pref**	pronoun agreement/reference error
comp	improper comparison	**ros**	run-on sentence, comma splice
d	diction, wrong word, part of speech	**sp**	spelling
frag	fragment; not a sentence	**s/v**	subject ≠ verb agreement
mm	misplaced or faulty modifier	**sub**	upside down ↔ subordination
nn	double negative	**t**	tense
#	number (*singular / plural*)	**ww**	wordy, repetitive, tautological
¶	paragraph		
//	parallel structure	**√**	correct, ok

1. _____ _____

A. To play violin well, several years' practice are required.
B. To play violin well, several years' practicing is required.
C. Playing violin well requires one to practice several years'.
D. To play violin well, one needs several years practice.
E. To play violin well, one needs to practice several years.

2. _____ _____

A. I think there can be no doubt that quitting smoking is difficult.
B. There can't be any doubt but that quitting smoking is difficult.
C. There can't be any doubting in that quitting smoking is difficult.
D. There can be no doubt but that quitting smoking is difficult.
E. There can be no doubt that quitting smoking is difficult, I don't think.

3. _____ _____

A. When entering the gallery, the woman's portrait seems to smile at us spectators.
B. When entering the gallery, the woman's portrait seems to smile at we spectators.
C. The woman's portrait seems to smile at we spectators when entering the gallery.
D. The woman's portrait seems to smile at us spectators when entering the gallery.
E. The woman's portrait on entering the gallery seems to smile at us spectators.

4. _____   _____

   A. Although in their 60s, both my mothers-in-law acted like they were 16 year olds.
   B. Although in their 60's, both my mother-in-laws acted as if they were 16 year olds.
   C. Although in their '60s, both my mother-in-laws acted like 16 year-olds.
   D. While in their '60s, nevertheless my mothers-in-law acted like they were 16 year olds.
   E. In their 60s, both my mothers-in-laws acted like 16 year-olds.

5. _____   _____

   A. I should like seeing you being present in class yesterday.
   B. I should have liked seeing you being present in class yesterday.
   C. I should have liked to see you in class yesterday.
   D. I should like to have seen you in class yesterday.
   E. I should like having seen you present in class yesterday.

6. _____   _____

   A. Every one of the players threw their hats in the air.
   B. Every one of the players threw their hat in the air.
   C. Every one of the players threw her hat in the air.
   D. Every one of the players threw their hats into the air.
   E. Every one of the players threw his hat into the air.

7. _____   _____

   A. Our actors prefer performing tragedies in winter comedy in summer.
   B. Our actors prefer to perform tragedies in winter, comedy in summer.
   C. Our actors prefer performing' tragedies in winter, comedy in summer.
   D. Our actors prefer performing wintery tragedies, summery comedies.
   E. Our actors prefer to perform tragedies in winter, comedies in summer.

8. _____   _____

   A. I like dancing with Doris's sister or else with whoever finds me attractive.
   B. I like dancing with Dorises sister or else with whoever finds me attractive.
   C. I like dancing with Doris's sister or with whomever finds me attractive.
   D. I like dancing with Doris's sister or with who else finds me attractive.
   E. I like dancing with Doris' sister or whomever finds me attractive.

9. _____   _____

   A. By eight o'clock the lights having dimmed, the milling, chattering crowd take its seats.
   B. By eight o'clock the lights having dimmed, the milling, chattering crowd take their seats.
   C. By eight o'clock the lights dimming, the chattering milling, crowd takes its seats.
   D. By eight o'clock the lights having dimmed, the milling, chattering crowd took its seats.

E. By eight o'clock the lights having dimmed, the milling, chattering crowd took their seats.

10. _____ _____

A. The longer anyone goes without eating, the more desperate you become.
B. The longer anyone goes without eating, the more desperate he becomes.
C. The longer someone goes without eating, the more desperate you become.
D. The longer one goes without eating, the more desperate one becomes.
E. The longer one went without eating, the more desperate one had become.

11. _____ _____

A. Three activities I like best are: ocean sailing, riding a dirt bike and to play croquet.
B. Three activities I like best are: to sail on the ocean, to ride a dirt bike and to play croquet.
C. Three activities I like best are: ocean sailing, riding a dirt bike and playing croquet.
D. Three activities I like best are: sailing on the ocean, riding a dirt bike, and playing croquet.
E. Three activities I like best are: to sail on the ocean, to ride a dirt bike, and playing croquet.

12. _____ _____

A. When just a toddler, my parents' divorce became official.
B. My parents' divorce became official; when I was just a toddler.
C. My parents divorce became official: I was just a toddler.
D. My parents divorce became official, when I was just a toddler.
E. When I was just a toddler, my parents' divorce became official.

13. _____ _____

A. If ever I am being lonely, I always had had you to rely on.
B. If ever I was lonely; I always had you to rely on.
C. If ever I was lonely, I always have had you to rely on.
D. If ever I were lonely, I always had you to rely on.
E. If ever I were lonely, I always had had you to rely on.

14. _____ _____

A. Besides seeing-eye dogs no pets are permitted inside of the fence.
B. Besides seeing-eye dogs no pets are permitted inside the fence.
C. Beyond seeing-eye dogs no pets are permitted inside the fence.
D. Beside seeing eye dogs no pet is permitted inside of the fence.
E. Beside seeing-eye dogs no pet is permitted inside the fence.

15. _____ _____

A. Boston is as cosmopolitan as Chicago, and more fun, big, and unpolluted than New York.
B. Boston is cosmopolitan a city as Chicago, and more fun, bigger, and has less pollution than New York.
C. Boston is as cosmopolitan as Chicago, and more fun, bigger, and less polluted than New York.
D. Boston is cosmopolitan like Chicago, and more fun, big, and less polluted than New York.

E. Boston is as cosmopolitan a city as Chicago; more fun, bigger, and less polluted than New York.

16. _____   _____

A. Baby-boomers seem more to prefer Springsteen's tunes and lyrics than the Beatles.
B. Baby-boomers seem to prefer more Springsteen's tunes and lyrics than the Beatles.
C. Baby-boomers seem to prefer Springsteen's tunes and lyrics more than the Beatles.
D. Baby-boomers seem to prefer Springsteen's tunes and lyrics to those of the Beatles'.
E. Baby-boomers seem to prefer Springsteen's tunes and lyrics to the Beatles'.

17. _____   _____

A. There's increasingly more ads on Internet sites and less of the songs I like to hear.
B. Increasingly more ads are on Internet sites and less of the songs I like to hear.
C. There is increasingly more ads on Internet sites and fewer of the songs I like to hear.
D. They're increasing ads on Internet sites and fewer of the songs I like to hear.
E. Increasingly more ads are on the Internet and fewer of the songs I like to hear.

18. _____   _____

A. Melville's book *Moby Dick* tells of Ahab's driven quest to avenge the loss of his leg.
B. Melville's book Moby Dick tells of Ahab's driven quest to avenge his lost leg.
C. In Melville's book "*Moby Dick*", it tells of Ahab's driven quest to avenge his loss of a leg.
D. Melville's book, *Moby Dick,* tells of Ahab's driven quest to avenge his loss of a leg.
E. Melville's book *Moby Dick* tells of Ahab's driven quest to revenge for his lost leg.

19. _____   _____

A. My baby sister is continuously slobbering on her bib during meals, which drives me crazy.
B. My baby sister is continually slobbering on her bib during meals, which drives me crazy.
C. My baby sister's continual slobbering on her bib during meals drives me crazy.
D. My baby sister continually slobbering on her bib during meals drives me crazy.
E. My baby sister's continuously slobbering on her bib during meals drive me crazy.

20. _____   _____

A. Neither her brothers nor her is admitting their fault in the bizaar accident.
B. Neither of her brothers nor she is admitting his or her fault in the bizarre accident.
C. Neither she nor her brothers is admitting fault in the bizarre accident.
D. Neither her brothers nor she herself is admitting their fault in the bizzare accident.
E. Neither she and nor her brothers are admitting their fault in the bizarre accident.

21. _____   _____

A. Personality is one criteria of judgement in the Miss World contest; however looks are crucial.
B. Personality is one criteria of judgement in the Miss World contest, however looks are crucial.
C. Personality is one criteria of judgment in the Miss World contest. Looks, however, are crucial.
D. Personality is one of the criteria of judgment in the Miss World contest. However, looks are crucial.

E. Personality is one of the judgment criteria in the Miss World contest; however, looks are crucial.

22. _____   _____

A. During spring break, we drove South to Florida, because it was warmer there.
B. During Spring break, we drove south to Florida, because it was warmer there.
C. During spring break, we drove South to Florida, where it was warmer.
D. During spring break, we drove south to Florida, because its weather was warmer.
E. Because its weather was warmer during spring break, we drove south to Florida.

23. _____   _____

A. Our boss's anger rose when he saw us leaving early.
B. Our boss's anger rose seeing our leaving early.
C. Our bosses anger rose seeing we were leaving early.
D. Our boss's anger rose seeing our having left earlier.
E. Our boss's anger rose in seeing us leaving early.

24. _____   _____

A. Miller's beer advertises it has more taste and less calories.
B. Miller Beer advertizes it has more taste and less calories.
C. Millers Beer is advertised with more taste and less calories.
D. Miller beer advertises it with more taste and fewer calories.
E. Miller advertises beer that has more taste and fewer calories.

25. _____   _____

A. Although my wife cheated on me and emptied my bank account, I still loved her.
B. My wife cheated on me, wasn't faithful, and emptied my bank account, although I still loved her.
C. My wife cheated on me, was unfaithful to me, and emptied out my bank account, but I still loved her.
D. Although I still loved her, my wife cheated on me and emptied my bank account.
E. My wife cheated on me, was unfaithful, and emptied my bank account, although I still loved her.

Answers

1. E   case   //   p   mm
2. A   mm   nn
3. D   case   mm

4. E   comp   d   sp   p
5. C   case   t
6. E   d   pref
7. E   pref   //   p   d
8. A   case   p

9. E   pref   s/v   t
10. D   pref   //   t
11. D   //   p
12. E   case   mm   p
13. D   frag   p   t

14. B   d   sp
15. C   comp   p   //   frag
16. E   case   comp   ww
17. E   d   pref   s/v
18. A   d   p   pref

19. C   d   p   s/v
20. B   comp   pref   sp   s/v   case   ww
21. E   #   p   sp
22. D   <u>c</u>   mm   pref
23. A   case   d   mm   t

24. E   <u>c</u>   d   mm   pref   sp   case   p
25. A   //   sub   ww

Practice Tests

Identifying Sentence Errors and *Improving Sentences* are deliberately formatted similarly to the verbal SAT.

The practice tests include the added task of assigning a standard Correction Code to each item, such that not only may an alphabetic letter <u>locate</u> a sentence problem, but a corresponding symbol may <u>identify</u> the specific abusage. It should be noted that the paragraphing ¶, capitalization *c*, and spelling *sp* symbols are not germane to the original exercise. In addition, depending on the nature of a word collection that constitutes a non-sentence, a group of fragments *frags* may be identified as a *ros* in the answer key. Should an error not exactly match with any correction symbols, mark the blank with an *x*.

Correction Symbols

case	(*nominative, possessive, objective*)	*p*	punctuation
c	capitalization	*pref*	pronoun agreement, vague reference
comp	improper comparison	*ros*	run-on sentence, comma splice
d	diction, wrong word, part of speech	*sp*	spelling
frag	fragment; not a sentence	*s/v*	subject ≠ verb agreement
mm	misplaced or faulty modifier	*sub*	upside down ↔ subordination
nn	double negative	*t*	tense
#	number (*singular/plural*)	*ww*	wordy, verbose, tautological
¶	paragraph		
//	parallel structure	√	ok, correct

Identifying Sentence Errors

Write the letter of the sentence A – D containing an error and the corresponding correction symbol. The letter E and the check mark symbol designate no error.

Identifying Sentence Errors I

1. The environmentalist <u>emphatically</u> detested
                           A
   the use of CFC's<u>, and they</u> have <u>been</u>
                   B
   <u>harming</u> the environment for <u>a half century</u>.
      C   D
   <u>No error.</u>
     E

2. Regardless of <u>their</u> credit history or what
                  A
   their prior housing arrangement <u>is</u>, the
                               B
   <u>tenants insisted</u> <u>that they could afford</u> to pay
       C   D
   for the apartment. <u>No error.</u>
                    E

3. Erin and Lisa <u>hoped to become</u> <u>a doctor</u>
                 A   B
   because <u>their</u> father was one of Mass
         C
   General's <u>most respected</u> doctors and
             D
   had healed over forty patients this year.

   <u>No error.</u>
     E

4. Neither Rutherford <u>or</u> Millikan <u>could have</u>
            A   B
   <u>predicted</u> the nature of the scientific study of

   Einstein, <u>who</u> <u>would later revolutionize</u>
           C   D
   quantum physics as a science. <u>No error.</u>
                                  E

5. Failure to do <u>one's</u> homework with proper
             A
   care <u>can cause</u> <u>you</u> to fall behind in school
        B   C
   and ultimately <u>to perform</u> poorly on
               D
   examinations proctored in school. <u>No error.</u>
                                    E

6. <u>Whenever</u> the bank teller <u>attempts to open</u>
       A   B
   the safe, she <u>must put</u> in the correct
                 C
   combination, then the six-digit pass code, and
   <u>then type in the correct password</u> before she
             D
   can get inside. <u>No error.</u>
                 E

7. <u>An intelligent computer programmer</u>, Bruce
            A
   Loce <u>suffers from paranoia</u>, <u>craziness</u>, and
           B   C
   <u>password-protects all</u> of his files. <u>No error.</u>
          D   E

8. The international summits, <u>attended by the</u>
                                    A
   <u>United States</u>, Great Britain, and Russia,
   <u>which has furthered</u> foreign relations
           B
   <u>among</u> the nations, <u>are held</u> annually in
     C   D
   Europe. <u>No error.</u>
            E

9. Trust <u>between</u> my mother and <u>me</u> has
         A   B
   <u>irreparably broke</u> because she knows that I
        C
   <u>had left</u> my room after midnight. <u>No error.</u>
     D   E

10. <u>Without a doubt</u>, the hardest task <u>in basic</u>
         A   B
    <u>training will be</u> the obstacle course <u>in the</u>
                                 C
    <u>woods and in the lake</u>. <u>No error.</u>
        D   E

11. Recent studies in sociology claim that not
                                        A
    sending children to daycare or other social
       B
    environments as young kids jeopardizes their
                                    C
    futures as a professional businessperson
             D
    No error.
    E

12. Democrats were outraged that the outcome
                                 A
    of the presidential race in 2000, which was
    decided by the Florida recounts, is not
        B   C
    favorable for their political positions. No
      D
    error.
    E

13. My uncle, who is a real estate appraiser,
                 A
    works real hard taking measurements and
          B   C
    driving to many locations all day and writing
       D
    reports at night. No error.
                      E

14. Being that she left her son alone in the car, the
        A
    woman was surprised that police were
          B   C
    waiting for her because, in the heat, the child
    had passed out from anoxia. No error.
        D   E

15. When Mary was asked by the teacher to
                 A
    choose Bernie or I for her partner, she
                    B
    responded that she did not want to choose
                C
    between her best friends and asked that the
    teacher choose for her. No error.
            D   E

16. My teacher insisted that we students take the
                           A
    time to purchase an SAT preparation book
          B
    and to study it diligently up until test day. No
            C   D
    error.
    E

17. My mother is always worried with my health,
                         A
    so she has me take a multivitamin every
    B   C
    morning and makes me go to the doctor once
                                           D
    every six months. No error.
                      E

18. Benjamin Franklin, a brilliant scientific mind
                       A
    of the Eighteenth Century, performed his
                               B
    famous key and kite experiment in a vastly,
           C
    open field. No error.
    D   E

Identifying Sentence Errors II

1. <u>Just weeks after</u> Ryan <u>moved</u> out of the
        A   B
   house, he found that <u>it is</u> hard to live alone,
                             C
   <u>so he</u> returned home. <u>No error.</u>
     D   E

2. <u>While walking</u> to the store, Joanna <u>stooped</u>
        A   B
   <u>in order to</u> tie her shoe <u>and found</u> a shiny
      C   D
   new quarter on the ground. <u>No error.</u>
                                 E

3. <u>It is</u> a difficult task to <u>choose</u> between <u>either</u>
     A   B   C
   Jim and George, but it is necessary for me <u>to</u>
                                        D
   <u>decide.</u> <u>No error.</u>
     D   E

4. Considering that the ancient civilization <u>has</u>
   <u>existed</u> for thousands of years, <u>it is</u> obvious
     A   B
   <u>they were</u> present <u>prior to</u> the Spanish
      C   D
   invasion in the 1600s. <u>No error.</u>
                           E

5. Scientists in Arizona <u>discovered recently</u> the
                                A
   remains of a rare dinosaur, the ixyasaur, <u>the</u>
   <u>only one</u> <u>of a kind</u> found <u>thus far.</u> <u>No error.</u>
     B   C   D   E

6. <u>Just as</u> some people rely on the computer for
     A
   <u>their</u> work, <u>so others</u> condemn <u>them</u> for
    B   C   D
   being too complex. <u>No error.</u>
                     E

7. Since John <u>is not found</u> when the searchers
                 A
   <u>went looking for him,</u> the citizens <u>are</u>
                                  B
   <u>forming</u> another group <u>in the hope that</u> they
     C   D
   will find him. <u>No error.</u>
               E

8. Edgar proposed that we should play tennis,
   <u>whereas</u> I believed that we <u>should play</u>
     A   B
   soccer because <u>more players</u> are able to play
                 C
   <u>at one time</u> in soccer than in tennis. <u>No error.</u>
     D   E

9. The teacher informed us <u>that tomorrow's test</u>
                           A
   would be not only be highly important,
   <u>but extremely</u> difficult, so <u>we should study</u>
     B   C
   <u>diligently.</u> <u>No error.</u>
     D   E

10. Just <u>between</u> you and <u>I,</u> Susan seems
         A   B
    <u>less qualified</u> than <u>she,</u> so I won't
      C   D
    support Susan for the job. <u>No error.</u>
      D   E

11. I encouraged them to try <u>eating spinach</u> and
                              A
    <u>drink</u> some herbal tea, <u>but they</u> were
      B   C
    apprehensive <u>and refused.</u> <u>No error.</u>
                  D   E

12. In a contest <u>between</u> our school and a visiting
            A
    school, the <u>home team</u> proved <u>best</u> at scoring.
                    C   D
    <u>No error</u>.
    E

13. <u>They were going</u> <u>to see</u> the new
         A   B
    Batman movie, starring Christian Bale <u>as</u>
                                             C
    the caped crusader, while their friends

    went to see the new *Star Wars* movie

    <u>that featured</u> Hayden Christenson and Natalie
         D
    Portman. <u>No error</u>
              E

14. <u>Owing to</u> his large girth and short stature,
         A
    Dan Gable, <u>an Olympian</u>, is <u>well suited to</u>
                    B   C
    <u>wrestling</u>. <u>No error</u>.
        D   E

15. Of China, Japan, <u>or</u> the US, in terms of
                      A
    wealth, America is <u>richer</u> and is likely to
                           B
    remain so <u>further</u> in the <u>foreseeable</u> future.
                  C   D
    <u>No error</u>.
        E

16. <u>Though</u> he was extremely <u>advanced in</u>
         A   B
    mathematics, the intelligent boy

    <u>nevertheless</u> found calculus to be <u>real</u>
          C   D
    hard. <u>No error</u>.
              E

17. The quality of an Oriental rug is

    determined <u>by how</u> finely <u>it's</u> individual
                   A   B
    threads are bound together and <u>by how</u>
                                        C
    resistant the rug is <u>to stains</u>. <u>No error</u>.
                              D   E

18. <u>Also vetoed</u> by the president <u>was</u> the bills
         A   B
    legalizing the death penalty and higher

    taxes <u>because</u>, when he was running for
              C
    president, he swore <u>to oppose such bills</u>.
                             D
    <u>No error</u>.
        E

Identifying Sentence Errors III

1. <u>After hurrying out the door</u> and trying <u>to make</u>
           A   B
   <u>it</u> to the bookstore <u>before it closes</u>,
                           C
   Chelsea and I unlawfully <u>sped</u> down
                                D
   the highway and received a ticket. <u>No
   error.</u>
     E

2. At a formal reception, arriving <u>too</u> late can be <u>worse</u>
                                   A   B
   <u>than</u> not <u>to show up</u> at all.
    C   D
   <u>No error.</u>
      E

3. My grandmother said that her <u>splitting</u>
                                      A
   headache <u>was not alleviated much</u> by <u>me</u>
                    B   C
   screaming and bawling <u>like a two-year</u>
                               D
   old. <u>No error.</u>
       E

4. <u>An indisputable literary genius,</u>
        A
   Shakespeare <u>wrote</u> many profound plays,
           B
   <u>moving sonnets,</u> <u>and died</u> as one
     C   D
   of the most influential playwrights of all
   time. <u>No error.</u>
       E

5. Molly and Sarah, <u>which</u> were two of the
           A
   most annoying <u>elementary school-age</u>
            B
   children <u>I've ever met</u>, matured to be
        C
   interesting, fun, <u>smart women</u>. <u>No error.</u>
           D   E

6. It is obvious <u>by simply comparing</u> the
          A
   two authors <u>that</u> Dickens writes much
          B
   <u>more wordier</u> than Harper Lee. <u>No error.</u>
    C   D   E

7. Dr. Phil advises that a substantial number
   of <u>family-time</u> hours <u>help</u> to reduce stress
    A   B
   in the household and to unite members
   <u>who would not be able</u> to see <u>each other</u>
    C   D
   otherwise. <u>No error.</u>
       E

8. Statistics show that <u>two out of every three</u>
           A
   kids <u>under the age of nine</u> do not include
           B
   enough calcium in <u>their</u> diets to provide
           C
   themselves <u>with the basis for</u> an
           D
   ideal bone structure. <u>No error.</u>
       E

9. <u>Just because</u> South Africa does not have
    A
   the economic or political influence <u>that</u>
   the United States <u>has</u> <u>does not mean</u> that
       B   C
   <u>they</u> should be excluded from the U.N.
    D
   <u>No error.</u>
     E

10. <u>All</u> of the history department's former
     A
    chairpersons, Dr. Rotundo, Dr.
    Henningsen and <u>me</u>, <u>decided to veto</u> Mr.
          B   C
    Gurry's request <u>for</u> an expanded
            D
    curriculum in History 200. <u>No error.</u>
        E

11. Fossilized remains of dinosaurs from the
        A   B
    Triassic period indicate that the triceratops
                         C
    was as long or longer than the
                   D
    tyrannosaurus rex. No error.
                        E

12. Dickens' novel *A Tale of Two Cities* was once
                                       A
    more widely read and more popular in
        B   C
    French high schools than Albert Camus.
                                D
    No error.
      E

13. Although my brother is very receptive to
    be criticized constructively, he hates it
     A   B
    when people denounce his work without
     C
    any hint of positive encouragement. No
     D
    error.
     E

14. The two main reasons for going to war
                          A
    with Iraq were the apparent threat of
            B
    weapons of mass destruction combined
    together with the dictatorial regime installed by
      C   D
    Saddam Hussein. No error.
                        E

15. It seems preposterous that such a sweet
                       A
    and innocent girl as her could commit an
                   B
    act so heinous and so cruel to Gregory and
                  C
    him. No error.
     D   E

16. Britney Spears' singing career has
        A
    skyrocketed since the initial release of her
        B   C
    album "Baby One More Time" in 1998,
    is still rising at an unprecedented rate. No
       D
    error.
     E

17. Cornell University has a world-renowned
                          A
    meteorology program, when the
                   B
    Massachusetts Institute of Technology
    continues to offer the greatest program in
      C   D
    physics. No error.
           E

18. The most pretty girl in the class, Tanya,
         A
    said that she had recently taken on a
          B   C
    boyfriend, and all of the boys claimed to
    be the one. No error.
      D   E

Identifying Sentence Errors IV

1. <u>Because of</u> his previous experience
      A
   <u>canoeing</u> in whitewater rapids, John
     B
   proved to be <u>as good</u> or <u>better than</u> the
                C   D
   trip leader. <u>No error.</u>
             E

2. Neither Eric <u>or</u> Greg <u>had heard that</u> the
             A   B
   circus <u>would be coming</u> to town for two
             C
   weeks, <u>starting</u> on the following Friday.
           D
   <u>No error.</u>
   E

3. Next to my <u>relatively</u> small closet <u>sets</u> a
            A   B
   huge chest of drawers and a picture of my
   family <u>that was taken</u> <u>on our trip</u> to
         C   D
   Europe last fall. <u>No error.</u>
             E

4. <u>When he asked</u>, I told my dad that I
     A
   wasn't hungry because I <u>had already ate</u> a
                      B
   <u>rather</u> large sub <u>earlier today</u>. <u>No error.</u>
     C   D   E

5. <u>When</u> you are lost in the woods, drinking
     A
   ample water and <u>finding sufficient food</u> <u>are</u>
                B   C
   necessary <u>in</u> your survival. <u>No error.</u>
          D   E

6. IBM promised to ship <u>their</u> new laptop
                     A
   to me <u>within</u> ten business days, but the unit
          B
   arrived at my doorstep <u>only</u> four days
                       C
   after it <u>had been purchased</u>. <u>No error.</u>
             D   E

7. Wanting to kill someone <u>who</u> annoys you
                         A
   is one thing; <u>to follow through</u> <u>with</u> your
                B   C
   impulses is <u>quite</u> another. <u>No error.</u>
            D   E

8. My piano teacher insisted that it was <u>they</u>
                                   A
   <u>who</u> she saw at the music store
     B
   <u>purchasing</u> Chopin's "Military Polonaise"
       C
   <u>the previous week</u>. <u>No error.</u>
       D   E

9. The band Metallica, <u>which</u> is known for
                   A
   <u>their</u> stance on anti-piracy laws, <u>will be</u>
     B
   <u>performing</u> a promotional concert this
       C
   Friday <u>on the Commons</u>. <u>No error.</u>
           D   E

10. As the set <u>came tumbling down</u> in the
                  A
    middle of the performance, <u>it became</u>
    <u>clear</u> that Jay, <u>who was employed</u> to
      B   C
    construct the scenery, had not rigged it in
    place <u>correct</u>. <u>No error.</u>
         D   E

11. To think and succeed is better than acting
         A   B   C
    rashly and to regret your actions. No error.
      D   E

12. Nike Corporation is known widely for its
                         A   B
    treatment of its employees in foreign
    countries, forcing them to work long hours,
                    C
    to slave in hot factories, and to receive
                                D
    inhumanely low wages. No error.
                          E

13. At the bottom of the Pacific Ocean lays the
                                      A
    mysterious Temple of Mu, whose colossal
                          B
    plazas are believed to have once sparkled
                  C
    with the pageantry of a vanished people. No
                       D
    error.
      E

14. Joan and Sarah, who are known for their
                  A   B
    tendency to shop until they had no more
                           C
    money, have not gone near a mall in over
            D
    four days. No error.
            E

15. Less than seven people have successfully
      A
    climbed Mount Everest, the tallest mountain
                              B
    in the world, because of its hostile climate
                C   D
    and insurmountable height. No error.
                            E

16. A linebacker blitz in football is where the
                                A
    defensive backs rush the quarterback, who's
                                     B
    then either tackled or hurries up the play.
          C   D
    No error.
        E

17. Yo Yo Ma, a renowned cellist, traveled
               A
    to many foreign countries abroad to perform
                            B
    concerts whose musical selections included
            C
    classical as well as traditional pieces. No error.
            D   E

18. Singer Mick Jagger, together with his band, are
                      A   B
    supposedly due to play here two weeks hence.
          C   D
    No error.
        E

Identifying Sentence Errors V

1. Several of the boys want to be a
A
professional baseball player when they
B C
are adults, but, as we all know, it is
D
unlikely that any of them will achieve this
goal. No error.
E

2. It is best to have a third party settle a
disagreement between two people, for the third
A B
party is most likely to settle the matter fair and
C D
justly. No error.
E

3. My father and myself were the proud
A
recipients of the family science fair award
for our research on the methods by which
B C
dolphins communicate with each other.
D
No error.
E

4. The theory of evolution, though it
A
contradicts many traditional religious
beliefs, has become accepted among
B C
scientific and religious figures alike.
D
No error.
E

5. My teacher liked the Rolling Stones' music
A
better than the Beatles; she had been raised
B C
by a father preferring Jagger's swagger to
D
McCartney's mellowness. No error.
E

6. In the lobby of the doctor's office is an
A
abundance of magazines, many of which
B C
discuss womens' interests, sports cars,
D
and current events. No error.
E

7. Tell doctors Haggard, Newman, and their nurse
A
that they're needed at once in the baby delivery
B D C
ward. No error.
E

8. Since newer technology has rendered my
A
computer obsolete, I had purchased a new
B C
processor to replace the old one. No error.
D E

9. Grace is an excellent writer, so when the
A
teacher read a marvelous essay without
B
revealing the author's identity, everyone
presumed it to be her. No error.
C D E

10. Those books on the shelf over there are
A B
medical manuals to discuss prescription
C
drugs and remedies using herbs. No error.
D E

11. Although one likes to think that your own
    A   B   C
    personality is flawless, others can be
    more objective about commenting on
    one's character traits. No error.
         D   E

12. Rayshawn can leap higher than any other boy
              A   B
    on his track and field team, however
                                C
    he was not chosen for the all-state
                             D
    competition. No error.
                  E

13. Mr. Blackwood asked his students whom
                                       A
    in their opinions would be the best
         B   C
    representatives for the class in the state
         D
    spelling bee. No error.
                   E

14. Bill Clinton reported to the public during
    his second term that he did not have an
         A   B
    inappropriate relationship with Monica
    Lewinsky but later admitting to having the
              C
    interaction and was impeached. No error.
                D   E

15. The coach insisted vehemently that each
                          A   B
    of the baseball players bring their own bat
                            C   D
    to the game. No error.
                  E

16. The word "peruse", meaning
                        A
    to scrutinize thoroughly, is so often misused in
         B
    writing that it has adapted a second
                    C
    definition that conveys the exact opposite
                             D
    idea. No error.
           E

17. In Europe, the consumption of alcohol is
    A   B
    greater than nicotine, marijuana, and opium
      C   D
    combined. No error.
               E

18. The tutor objected to the student simply
                        A
    sitting in the chair all day and refusing to do
         B   C
    any work in preparation for the SAT. No
              D
    error.
    E

Identifying Sentence Errors VI

1. My father warned me to drive <u>slow</u> on the
                                        A
   back roads of Plymouth <u>because</u> they are
                                 B
   <u>very narrow</u> and because people walk in
       C
   the middle <u>of them</u>. <u>No error.</u>
                D   E

2. Make sure <u>to remind</u> James and <u>me</u> of
                  A   B
   <u>Nicole</u> arriving after she steps off
     C
   her plane and <u>retrieves her luggage from</u>
                           D
   baggage claim. <u>No error.</u>
                      E

3. I rode my bicycle <u>off of</u> a ramp <u>and</u>
                    A
   <u>scraped</u> my knees, <u>which</u> caused me pain
    B   C
   for the next three weeks <u>while I was in</u>
                             D
   recovery. <u>No error.</u>
            E

4. <u>Losing</u> at the battle of Waterloo
     A
   in 1815, <u>Napoleon's empire</u> collapsed
             B
   <u>within</u> a <u>matter of days</u> in a crushing
    C   D
   defeat. <u>No error.</u>
          E

5. My dad always says <u>that if</u> he <u>was</u> in charge,
                   A   B
   <u>undoubtedly</u> he would eradicate poverty
      C
   in destitute nations <u>such as many of</u>
                     D
   those in Africa. <u>No error.</u>
                 E

6. Scott Joplin, the pioneer of <u>the musical</u>
                              A
   genre ragtime, <u>had composed</u> <u>over</u> one
                 B   C
   hundred original rags, <u>inclusive</u> the
                     D
   "Maple Leaf Rag" and "The Entertainer".
   <u>No error.</u>
    E

7. Although <u>its</u> delivery was slated for
          A
   Thursday <u>by</u> 4:30 P.M., the package
          B
   arrived <u>sooner than expected</u>, <u>being</u>
            C   D
   come at noon on Wednesday. <u>No error.</u>
                              E

8. Most teachers aspire to become <u>a role</u>
                                 A
   <u>model</u> for <u>their</u> students as well as <u>to</u>
             B
   <u>impart</u> to them useful knowledge and <u>life</u>
    C   D
   <u>skills.</u> <u>No error.</u>
          E

9. For <u>his</u> twelfth birthday party, <u>Jacob's</u>
       A   B
   <u>mother</u> decided to throw a surprise party
   hosted at the carnival<u>, consequently</u> he felt
                                    C
   <u>supremely</u> embarrassed. <u>No error.</u>
      D   E

10. Since <u>her</u> order was improperly executed,
          A
    Hilary requested to speak to <u>whomever</u>
                                   B
    <u>was</u> in charge of <u>shipping</u> merchandise.
     C   D
    <u>No error.</u>
       E

11. <u>Because of</u> the <u>media hype</u> and constant
    A   B
    <u>advertising</u> for the new movie "Charlie
    C
    and the Chocolate Factory", we thought
    that the movie <u>will be</u> fantastic. <u>No error.</u>
                   D   E

12. For the longest time, the teacher was <u>so</u>
    <u>absorbed</u> in <u>lecturing</u> the class <u>that</u> she
    A   B   C
    failed to notice the girl in back <u>which</u> had
                                      D
    her hand raised. <u>No error.</u>
                     E

13. Everybody laughed at <u>Cassie</u> <u>walking her</u>
                         A   B
    <u>rabbit</u>, the latest idea in a string of
    peculiar activities <u>in which</u> the Friedman
                        C
    family <u>has recently participated</u>. <u>No error.</u>
           D   E

14. <u>As he was unable to decide</u> between
    A
    cherry <u>or</u> orange on his own, Peter flipped
           B
    a coin <u>to assist him</u> <u>in</u> making the
           C   D
    decision. <u>No error.</u>
              E

15. My dad <u>is of the opinion</u> that Frogger, a
           A
    game <u>for the computer</u>, is quite a
         B
    ridiculous and pointless waste of time for
    a young child, <u>whose</u> studying and homework
                   C
    <u>is</u> far more crucial. <u>No error.</u>
    D   E

16. My teacher was <u>aggravated</u> by <u>my</u>
                    A   B
    <u>having arrived</u> late to class on four
    C
    <u>sequential</u> days. <u>No error.</u>
    D   E

17. Ray Kurzweil, the author of *The Age of*
    Spiritual Machines, <u>graduated</u> MIT <u>in the</u>
                          A   B
    <u>1970's</u> and <u>is now developing</u> voice
                     C
    recognition technology for leading
    <u>software producers.</u> <u>No error.</u>
    D   E

18. Antarctica, which is <u>larger than</u> <u>either</u>
                         A   B
    Europe or Australia in land area, houses
    <u>much less</u> life forms <u>because of</u> its
    C   D
    harsh, freezing climate. <u>No error.</u>
                             E

Identifying Sentence Errors VII

1. During the conquest of the Yucatan
    A   B
   Peninsula, Cortez and his army decimated

   the existing Mayan and Aztec
       C
   civilizations, pillaging their villages. No
                    D
   error.
    E

2. I had already wrote down the answers on
       A
   my response sheet when I realized that I
                      B   C
   was working on the wrong section. No
                 D
   error.
    E

3. To take a mulligan in a professional golf
                      A
   tournament is just acting dishonestly. No
                 B   C   D
   error.
    E

4. A hurricane is when turbulent winds
                   A
   combine with evaporation from warm tropical
       B
   waters to produce a destructive storm. No
          C   D
   error.   E

5. The tiger growled so fierce that, even
                           A
   though he was locked in a cage, he still
     B   C
   scared the children from behind his bars.
                          D
   No error.
      E

6. Children who live with only one parent
                                      A
   still appear, on average, to be more
                    B
   happier than those who live in foster
      C   D
   homes. No error.
              E

7. If you structure your argument in a clear,

   coherent, and logical manner, using plenty of
        A   B
   evidence that supports your thesis, you

   should earn a good grade. No error.
       C   D   E

8. It appears that there are a series of nine
        A   B
   more etymology books to complete once I
                        C
   finish learning the words in this
       D
   one. No error.
           E

9. George Bush has been known to speak
                    A   B
   publicly in a grammatically incorrect

   way, to slur speech, and to fail to
          C
   enunciate, which generates negativity
                  D
   from his critics. No error.
                        E

10. When you are sick with influenza, your body
     A   B
    temperature commonly raises three to five
                           C   D
    degrees Fahrenheit. No error.
                            E

11. In the mythical space adventures of *Star Wars*, the original Jedi <u>supposedly</u> have
                                    A
    been <u>trained and taught</u> <u>to use</u> light sabers
              B   C
    <u>by Yoda himself</u>. <u>No error</u>.
          D   E

12. Far <u>away from</u> <u>having invented</u>
         A   B
    transcontinental communication, Samuel
    Morse created Morse Code, <u>a language of</u>
                                    C
    communication <u>using a telegraph</u>. <u>No error</u>.
                        D   E

13. <u>For</u> the past 227 years, Phillips Academy
    A
    <u>stood</u> as the oldest and <u>most prestigious</u>
     B   C
    preparatory school <u>in the nation</u>. <u>No error</u>.
                            D   E

14. Of the two building options <u>that you have</u>
                                      A
    presented to me <u>thus far</u>, this one is <u>far and
                         B   C
    away</u> the best. <u>No error</u>.
      D   E

15. <u>Every time that</u> my brother steals my
         A
    baseball, I wish <u>that I could</u> retaliate, but
                          B
    because he is bigger than <u>me</u>, I am
                                  C
    <u>helpless</u>. <u>No error</u>.
        D   E

16. <u>Yelling at</u> one's parents <u>before going</u> to the
         A   B
    mall is a good way to ensure that they <u>will
                                              C
    not be buying you</u> anything. <u>No error</u>.
         C   D   E

17. <u>Although</u> <u>they had graduated</u> the previous
        A   B
    year, the two young alumni still
    <u>frequented campus</u> <u>like</u> they were current
          C   D
    students. <u>No error</u>.
                  E

18. The runner, seeing the finishing line 200
    yards <u>farther</u> ahead, could <u>not help thinking</u>
             A   B
    that, <u>but</u> for the wind, he <u>might win</u>. <u>No error</u>.
           C   D   E

Identifying Sentence Errors VIII

1. If you <u>would look</u> <u>behind</u> the counter, you
         A   B
   will find that <u>there are</u> a pile of books
                 C
   <u>written about</u> SAT preparation. <u>No error.</u>
      D   E

2. The most important thing <u>to keep in mind</u>
                                    A
   <u>when operating</u> the lawnmower is not
      B
   <u>going</u> at excessively high speeds, <u>for</u> the
     C   D
   motor could burn out. <u>No error.</u>
                          E

3. The pilot asked <u>everybody</u> on the plane
                    A
   to take <u>their</u> seat, relax, and not sit or
           B
   <u>lie</u> down in the aisles <u>during the flight</u>.
    C   D
   <u>No error.</u>
      E

4. Part of the reason <u>why</u> the thief passed
                      A
   the lie detector test <u>was</u> a <u>striking</u> ability
                    B   C
   to act <u>calm and collected.</u> <u>No error.</u>
           D   E

5. <u>The pieces</u> of your Monopoly game <u>is</u>
       A   B
   spread all over the floor and <u>will likely be</u>
                                    C
   picked up <u>by the vacuum cleaner.</u> <u>No</u>
               D
   error.
     E

6. Just when we thought we <u>were going</u> to
                            A
   get away with it, my mom <u>comes</u>
                             B
   by and <u>caught</u> us <u>right in the middle</u> of
          C   D
   the act. <u>No error.</u>
              E

7. The approval <u>ratings for</u> our program
                   A
   <u>have</u> been neither up to our own
    B
   standards <u>or</u> satisfactory to the producer,
            C
   <u>so</u> our show is being canceled. <u>No error.</u>
    D   E

8. In "Peter Pan", Tinkerbelle <u>saved</u> Peter's life
                             A
   <u>by drinking</u> poison <u>that</u> Captain Hook
      B   C
   <u>has meant evilly</u> for his boyish rival.
        D
   <u>No error.</u>
      E

9. <u>Before having left</u> for the beach, Nicole
        A
   forgot <u>to pack</u> our lunches, so we <u>were</u>
          B
   <u>left</u> <u>going hungry.</u> <u>No error.</u>
    C   D   E

10. Give either Joan <u>or</u> <u>I</u> the money <u>that is</u>
                   A B   C
    owed to us <u>from</u> our trip to the mall last
              D
    night. <u>No error.</u>
            E

11. Before <u>immigrating</u> to America, the family
          A
    <u>had had</u> a life of misery, with not enough
      B
    to eat, <u>to wear</u>, or <u>have to drink</u>. <u>No error.</u>
              C   D   E

12. My mother always objects to <u>me</u> staying
                                  A
    <u>up late, and</u> she <u>claims</u> that if I do, then I will
        B   C
    not grow <u>big and strong</u>. <u>No error.</u>
                  D   E

13. Our football opponents <u>proved</u> <u>to be</u> much
                              A   B
    better disciplined, practiced, and
    <u>equipped</u> than <u>us</u>. <u>No error.</u>
       C   D   E

14. <u>Irregardless of how</u> they made <u>fortunes</u>,
            A   B
    both Bill Gates, <u>working in</u> the highly
                         C
    respected technology field, and John
    Gotti of the notorious Mafia, are both
    strategic business men <u>who get what they</u>
                                    C
    want done. <u>No error.</u>
                    E

15. To add fractions of <u>unlike</u> denominators,
                            A
    <u>simply find</u> the least common
        B
    denominator, add the numerators, and
    <u>placing</u> the sum <u>over</u> the least common
        C   D
    denominator. <u>No error.</u>
                       E

16. <u>Twain's</u> writing is <u>more comical</u>, more fun,
        A   B
    and <u>easier</u> to read than <u>Hawthorne</u>. <u>No error.</u>
            C   D   E

17. There are many <u>less</u> words in the Spanish
                       A
    and French <u>languages</u> <u>than there</u> are in
                    B   C
    English <u>by a long shot</u>. <u>No error.</u>
                  D   E

18. One must be careful <u>when lifting</u> and
                              A
    transporting <u>either heavy or large</u> boxes
                          B
    containing fragile merchandise, so that
    <u>you</u> do not get hurt or <u>hurt</u> the contents of
     C   D
    the packages. <u>No error.</u>
                        E

Identifying Sentence Errors IX

1. <u>In my opinion</u>, I think that Mme.
      A
   Joseph, our French teacher, <u>whose</u> hair is
                                B
   always <u>a mess</u>, is an <u>active and engaging</u>
          C   D
   educator. <u>No error</u>.
               E

2. These <u>type</u> of flowers are preferable to that
         A
   <u>because of</u> a prettier color, a pleasing
     B
   scent, and an <u>ability to grow</u> in <u>almost any</u>
                  C   D
   greenhouse facility. <u>No error</u>.
                         E

3. <u>Us</u> accountants <u>should know better</u> than
    A   B
   <u>to spend lavishly</u>; <u>one</u> should invest
       C   D
   wisely and save up for retirement. <u>No
   error</u>.
    E

4. Before <u>the advent of</u> the modern telephone,
          A
   <u>sending</u> letters or telegrams <u>were considered</u>
     B   C
   to be the <u>cheapest and most practical</u> means
               D
   of communication. <u>No error</u>.
                   E

5. <u>Most</u> of the doctors <u>which</u> attended the
     A   B
   seminar <u>felt that</u> the speaker presented <u>in a</u>
           C   D
   <u>too</u> authoritative, dismissive manner. <u>No
   error</u>.
    E

6. <u>While flying</u> to Switzerland last June, I <u>had</u>
       A
   <u>read</u> all of my summer <u>reading required</u> for
    B   C
   those students <u>who</u> would start prep school
                   D
   in the fall. <u>No error</u>.
              E

7. The decorator <u>had</u> already mounted and <u>hung</u>
           A   B
   five abstract paintings before he <u>noticed</u> that
                                C
   three were <u>hanged</u> upside-down. <u>No error</u>.
            D   E

8. <u>After</u> an exhausting afternoon <u>of hiking up</u>
    A   B
   his favorite mountain, Jack <u>laid</u> down on his
                              C
   bed to take a nap <u>before he had to</u> turn
                      D
   around and make dinner. <u>No error</u>.
                         E

9. The <u>imminent</u> and <u>scholarly</u> writer John
         A   B
   Updike <u>now</u> has his own column in the
          C
   <u>world-renowned</u> New Yorker Magazine.
                D
   <u>No error</u>.
     E

10. <u>The more historians study</u> the life of George
            A
    Washington, the <u>more closely</u> they come to
                       B
    uncovering the <u>true nature of his presidency</u>
                             C
    and <u>the ways in which</u> he helped to shape
                D
    this country. <u>No error</u>.
                 E

11. Edwin Abbott was not only a profound
                    A   B
    mathematician but also a talented writer
                   C
    as well. No error.
    D   E

12. Lately, I have been unable to determine
    A   B
    what Brian is saying to me because
    he always says things so quick. No
                C   D
    error.
    E

13. Julia playing with the curls in her hair
    A
    distracted me, as usual, and it not only
                   B
    annoyed me but seemed as if it were
                          C   D
    intended to. No error.
                 E

14. Studying for years the nature of black holes,
    A
    scientists' speculations on the matter
    B
    suggest these phenomena may arise from giant
    C   D
    collapsed stars. No error.
                    E

15. Why is it that your acting so disgruntled
    A   B
    toward me about my decision to enroll you in
    C   D
    summer school? No error.
                   E

16. The new processor will be able to send and
                      A
    to receive data at rates as fast or faster than
    B   C
    last year's model, which ran at over 3.2
                      D
    gigahertz. No error.
              E

17. A parietal is where a person living in a dorm
              A
    facility asks his or her house counselor for
                   B
    permission to have a person of the opposite
               C
    sex unsupervised with him or her in his or
        D
    her room. No error.
              E

18. The common cold, which has over two
                     A
    hundred known strands, can be spread by
                          B
    coughing, sneezing, or if you share food or
                        C
    drink with someone who is infected. No
                        D
    error.
    E

Identifying Sentence Errors X

1. <u>Nearly everyone</u> in the class <u>agreed to</u>
        A   B
   Dan's viewpoint, for it was logically
   thought out, <u>well substantiated</u>, and
                        C
   forcefully <u>presented</u>. <u>No error.</u>
                 D   E

2. Of all the tragedies <u>of the recent past</u>, the
                               A
   deaths of over three thousand innocent
   people in the <u>attacks on</u> the World Trade
                  B
   Towers <u>was</u> by far the <u>most startling</u>. <u>No
         C   D
   error.</u>
   E

3. My mother <u>vehemently</u> objects to <u>my</u>
                A
   <u>brother</u> <u>playing baseball</u> in the house <u>with</u>
     B   C   D
   his friends. <u>No error.</u>
                   E

4. Robin Hood's <u>rule of thumb</u> <u>has always</u>
                  A   B
   <u>been</u> to steal money <u>from the wealthy</u> and
                      C
   to redistribute it to <u>whomever</u> needs it.
                        D
   <u>No error.</u>
   E

5. All of the <u>principals</u> of writing <u>are</u>
           A   B
   presented in the interns' English language
   series, <u>which outlines</u> <u>the basics of</u>
          C   D
   grammar, style, composition, and usage.
   <u>No error.</u>
     E

6. The internet <u>contains billions</u> of websites,
                   A
   including millions of <u>new ones</u> that are
                         B
   added every day, <u>which</u> range <u>from</u>
                            C
   <u>internet games to business advertisements</u>.
                       D
   <u>No error.</u>
   E

7. <u>Among</u> the choices <u>to get paid</u> or to work
    A   B
   <u>at community service</u> for free, I must
           C
   choose <u>to earn money</u> because I am
           D
   expected to pay for college in the fall. <u>No
   error.</u>
   E

8. The <u>new Prius cars</u>, manufactured by
        A
   Toyota, burn fuel <u>without leaving hardly</u>
                               B
   a trace <u>of poisonous</u> greenhouse gases <u>in</u>
           C   D
   the atmosphere. <u>No error.</u>
                     E

9. <u>Ultimately</u>, it is not important which side
     A
   of the argument you <u>advocate, you</u> will
                            B
   still earn a good grade as long as <u>it is</u> well
                                 C
   thought out and <u>buttressed</u> with good
                   D
   evidence. <u>No error.</u>
             E

10. The original manuscript of F. Scott Fitzgerald's *The Great Gatsby* <u>shows</u> (A) little <u>attention in</u> (B) proper grammar use although the natural <u>eloquence for</u> (C) and <u>feel with which</u> (D) Fitzgerald writes English words has often been compared by scholars to perfect pitch. <u>No error.</u> (E)

11. <u>I want</u> (A) to work out <u>our</u> (B) problems and <u>to move on</u> (C) with our relationship before our issues get <u>hopelessly out of hand.</u> (D) <u>No error.</u> (E)

12. Just between <u>you and I,</u> (A) I feel <u>as though</u> (B) the vice president-elect is <u>perhaps</u> (C) not as <u>well qualified</u> (D) as some of the other members of our current administration. <u>No error.</u> (E)

13. It <u>would be</u> (A) a good idea <u>to sit</u> (B) this delicate vase down in your china closet <u>before</u> (C) a little kid <u>runs into the porcelain</u> (D) and breaks it. <u>No error.</u> (E)

14. The Great Pyramids of Egypt, <u>which are</u> (A) level to a hundredth of an inch and stand <u>many hundreds</u> (B) of feet tall, <u>are said</u> (C) to be <u>a Wonder of the World.</u> (D) <u>No error.</u> (E)

15. <u>Doctors</u> (A) say <u>that</u> (B) one should take one multivitamin in the morning with your breakfast, but I always take two <u>to make</u> (C) sure I am <u>more than sufficiently</u> (D) nourished and energized. <u>No error.</u> (E)

16. Tom Cruise, <u>whose</u> (A) twenty-third film was "Minority Report" - <u>which premiered</u> (B) in 2002 - <u>and since then having produced</u> (C) five more, <u>one of which</u> (D) earned him an Oscar Nomination. <u>No error.</u> (E)

17. <u>Even though</u> (A) the denunciation of the project was addressed to the whole team <u>of innovators,</u> (B) I <u>couldn't help but feel</u> (C) the boss had aimed his criticisms at <u>you and me</u>. (D) <u>No error.</u> (E)

18. <u>After the show,</u> (A) <u>it</u> (B) was clear the three large men, who <u>were obviously bullying</u> (C) the small, frail man in front of them, <u>were going to be</u> (D) arrested. <u>No error.</u> (E)

Identifying Sentence Errors XI

1. The conglomeration of larger
   <u>A</u>
   corporations <u>may create a useful synergy</u>,
                    B
   <u>but the result</u> is often forcing <u>them to lay off</u>
         C   D
   workers. <u>No error.</u>
                 E

2. <u>By far</u> the best player on our soccer team,
      A
   Pablo is <u>undoubtedly</u> <u>better than</u>
                  B   C
   <u>any soccer player</u> in the state. <u>No error.</u>
          D   E

3. <u>Although</u> I attempted to awaken Matilda
      A
   during the middle of the night, she was
   not able to hear <u>me</u> knocking on her
                      B
   window because <u>it was</u> <u>so quiet.</u> <u>No error.</u>
                        C   D   E

4. <u>Don't tell</u> me that you do not know the
      A
   man <u>whom</u> I am talking about! He is <u>as</u>
           B
   <u>famous or more famous</u> than <u>anyone else</u>
            C   D
   in history! <u>No error.</u>
                    E

5. <u>In the study of mathematics</u> <u>there is</u> two
              A   B
   different types <u>of geometry</u> – Euclidean
                          C
   <u>and</u> spherical. <u>No error.</u>
      D   E

6. <u>Whenever I try</u> <u>to get the high score</u>
        A   B
   in my new video game, my brother, <u>the</u>
   <u>obnoxious rat</u>, bothers me <u>incessantly</u> and
         C   D
   ruins my concentration. <u>No error.</u>
                                E

7. <u>Because of</u> my medical condition,
        A
   asthma<u>, I am unable</u> <u>to play</u> sports
               B   C
   without bringing an inhaler <u>in case of</u> an
                                      D
   emergency. <u>No error.</u>
                    E

8. <u>Once in a great while</u>, my mom borrows
          A
   money <u>off of me,</u> but she <u>always</u> repays
              B   C
   me <u>in a timely fashion</u>. <u>No error.</u>
             D   E

9. <u>Doctors say</u> that one should exercise <u>three to</u>
       A   B
   <u>four</u> times per week to keep in shape, but
   I exercise <u>nearly every day</u> to keep in <u>tip-</u>
                      C
   <u>top shape.</u> <u>No error.</u>
        D   E

10. I was surprised that we did not <u>get cheated</u>
                                         A
    <u>when</u> we purchased a computer at the
      B
    computer show, <u>but instead</u> we received a
                         C
    great computer at a <u>real good</u> price. <u>No</u>
                              D
    <u>error.</u>
       E

11. Once you have cleaned the kitchen, <u>Nell,</u>
                                             A
    <u>than</u> you can sweep the hardwood floors
     B
    <u>of the downstairs</u> <u>and vacuum the carpets</u>.
         C   D
    <u>No error.</u>
      E

12. Please inform Eugene <u>that</u> he must decide
                                 A
    between <u>granting the interns</u> exclusive
                  B
    rights to the files on the main server <u>or</u>
                                      C
    <u>decreasing productivity</u>. <u>No error.</u>
         D   E

13. Each president appoints <u>their</u> own cabinet
                            A
    members, <u>who</u> are responsible <u>for</u>
            B   C
    advising the president on important issues

    <u>and helping him</u> to make executive
         D
    decisions. <u>No error.</u>
            E

14. <u>In spite of</u> the numerous interruptions <u>by</u>
       A   B
    annoying phone solicitations and his

    wife, <u>still</u> Brad <u>managed to get</u> his work
        C   D
    done on time. <u>No error.</u>
                 E

15. In my magazine <u>it says that</u> <u>one</u> can lose
                      A   B
    <u>up to thirty pounds</u> in thirty days,
              C
    <u>guaranteed.</u> <u>No error.</u>
        D   E

16. <u>In spite of</u> his <u>averse</u> circumstances,
       A   B
    wheelchair Johnny is determined to win a

    race because he is one of those people

    <u>determined to succeed,</u> <u>no matter</u>
                                 C
    <u>what any cynic says.</u> <u>No error.</u>
           D   E

17. It is crucial to the <u>well-being</u> of society
                       A
    that <u>there be</u> a welfare office that <u>helps</u>
         B   C
    <u>assisting</u> for a short period of time people

    who are needy. <u>No error.</u>
                  D   E

18. <u>For</u> the grass to receive a <u>healthy</u>
      A   B
    <u>watering,</u> it is necessary <u>to run</u> each
                              C
    underground sprinkling zone <u>for forty-</u>

    <u>five minutes each morning.</u> <u>No error.</u>
              D   E

Identifying Sentence Errors XII

1. The Andover meter maid, <u>by general consensus agreement</u> the most <u>unlikable</u> official of the town, <u>cruises up and down</u> Main Street every day, <u>waiting to hand out</u> tickets. <u>No error</u>.
   A .... B .... C .... D .... E

2. Burt said that he heard <u>me</u> screaming in the hallway and that, <u>as a result</u>, he <u>could not</u> <u>concentrate on</u> his work. <u>No error</u>.
   A .... B .... C .... D .... E

3. The Great Pyramids still <u>had stood</u> <u>over</u> two thousand years <u>after</u> the ancient Egyptians erected <u>them</u>. <u>No error</u>.
   A .... B .... C .... D .... E

4. The larger, <u>more bulky</u> football player asked me to <u>except</u> his <u>sincerest</u> apologies after he knocked me <u>flat on my face</u>. <u>No error</u>.
   A .... B .... C .... D .... E

5. My mother <u>continuously</u> reminds <u>me</u> to do my homework and <u>sounds like a broken record</u>, even if the work is not due the next day. <u>No error</u>.
   A .... B .... C .... D .... E

6. The modulation dial <u>on a radio</u> <u>is essential</u> <u>being that</u> it controls the station <u>to which one</u> is listening. <u>No error</u>.
   A .... B .... C .... D .... E

7. <u>Some</u> scientists argue that a male receives <u>the structure of the genetics</u> <u>who control</u> his appearance from <u>his</u> father. <u>No error</u>.
   A .... B .... C .... D .... E

8. Johnny, <u>who wanted</u> <u>to prove</u> that he was <u>different than</u> all the other boys in reform school, <u>behaved well</u> so that he might be able to get out early. <u>No error</u>.
   A .... B .... C .... D .... E

9. <u>More</u> students are applying to universities and colleges <u>seeking</u> early action or early decisions, and, as a result, <u>less</u> of them <u>have to apply to</u> multiple schools. <u>No error</u>.
   A .... B .... C .... D .... E

10. When <u>one</u> compares the works of Georges Seurat to <u>Leonardo Da Vinci</u>, <u>one</u> finds that the two artists embrace <u>largely disparate</u> styles. <u>No error</u>.
    A .... B .... C .... D .... E

11. Because neither of the students <u>are</u> old
                                     A
    enough <u>to drive</u> and <u>because</u> they can't take
            B   C
    the bus, their older sister, Jacqui, <u>has to</u>
                                          D
    <u>drive</u> them to school every morning.

    <u>No error</u>.
       E

12. <u>To be</u> an intern <u>in an organization</u> <u>is when</u>
       A   B   C
    you go to work for it, either for free or for a
    salary, and <u>in doing so</u> learn the ropes of
                   D
    running the business as well. <u>No error</u>.
                                     E

13. Nietzsche believed that a person's essence <u>is</u>
                                                A
    preceded by his existence and that a person
    is entirely responsible for his own actions,
    <u>being able</u> <u>to be defined</u> <u>only</u> by the sum of
        B   C   D
    his own decisions. <u>No error</u>.
                          E

14. <u>Which</u> musical piece <u>is</u> the <u>longest</u> – the
       A   B   C
    "Moonlight Sonata" <u>by Beethoven</u> or
                           D
    Chopin's "Minute Waltz?" <u>No error</u>.
                                E

15. <u>Some primary functions of platelets</u>,
                    A
    independent of a person's blood type, <u>are</u> to
                                           B
    help <u>controlling</u> bleeding and <u>to assist in</u>
            C   D
    blood clotting. <u>No error</u>.
                       E

16. <u>Realizing that</u> we had been working hard <u>at</u>
        A   B
    roofing the house <u>all day</u>, the homeowner
                         C
    offered Dustin and <u>me</u> a drink and a rest
                         D
    period. <u>No error</u>.
               E

17. Indiana Jones's <u>aversion with</u> snakes <u>never</u>
                        A   B
    prevents him and Marion <u>from escaping</u>
                                  C
    from a pit full of asps <u>in the first episode</u>,
                                 D
    Raiders of the Lost Ark. <u>No error</u>.
                                  E

18. <u>As tempting as</u> your offer <u>to provide</u> me with
        A   B
    a substantial year-end bonus <u>sounds</u>, I must
                                    C
    <u>respectably</u> decline your offer to take a job
        D
    that allows me to work closer to my home.

    <u>No error</u>.
       E

Answers

Corrections Symbols have been supplied as an aid to understanding the errors identified by letter in the first six sets of "Identifying Sentence Errors". Supply the requisite symbols for sections VII – XII.

Sentence Error Answers I - III

Sentence Errors I	Sentence Errors II	Sentence Errors III
1. B CFCs sp	1. C was t	1. C t
2. B was t	2. E √	2. D //
3. B doctors #	3. C ~~either~~ ww	3. C case
4. A nor comp	4. C it was pref	4. C //
5. C one pref	5. C its kind d	5. A pref
6. D ~~type in~~ //	6. D it pref	6. C comp
7. C acts crazy //	7. A was t	7. B s/v
8. B have s/v	8. E √	8. E √
9. C broken t	9. B but also comp	9. D pref
10. E √	10. B me case	10. B case
11. D a person**s** #	11. B drink**ing** //	11. D comp
12. C was t	12. D better comp	12. D comp
13. B really d	13. D featuring //	13. A t
14. A Since she t	14. E √	14. C ww
15. B me case	15. B richest comp	15. B case
16. D ~~up~~ d	16. D really d	16. D frag
17. A ~~with~~ about d	17. B it**s** p	17. B ww
18. D vast d	18. B were s/v	18. A comp

Sentence Error Answers IV - VI

Sentence Errors IV	Sentence Errors V	Sentence Errors VI
1. C good **as** comp	1. B a….players #	1. A slow**ly** d
2. A nor comp	2. D fair**ly** d	2. C Nicole**'s** case
3. B sits d	3. A I pref	3. C and that pref
4. B eaten t	4. E √	4. B After the loss mm
5. D ~~in~~ to d	5. B Beatles' comp	5. B were t
6. A its pref	6. D women's sp	6. D inclusive **of** d
7. B following //	7. E √	7. D having d
8. B whom case	8. C ~~had~~ t	8. A role models #
9. B its pref	9. E √	9. C . Consequently ros
10. D correct**ly** d	10. C discussing t	10. B whoever case
11. C to act ~~ing~~ //	11. C one's own pref	11. D would be t
12. E √	12. C ; p	12. D who/that pref
13. A lies d	13. A who case	13. A Cassie**'s** case
14. C have t	14. C admitted t	14. B or and d
15. A Fewer #	15. D his pref	15. D are s/v
16. A occurs if d	16. C adopted d or sp	16. A irritated d
17. B ~~abroad~~ ww	17. D than that of comp	17. A graduated <u>from</u> d
18. B is s/v	18. A student**'s** case	18. C many fewer #

Sentence Answers Tests VII - IX

Sentence Errors VII	Sentence Errors VIII	Sentence Errors IX
1. E √	1. C s/v	1. A ww
2. A t	2. C //	2. A #
3. C //	3. B pref	3. A case
4. A pref	4. D d	4. C s/v
5. A d	5. B s/v	5. B pref
6. C comp	6. B t	6. B t
7. E √	7. C comp	7. D d
8. B s/v	8. A t	8. C d
9. D pref	9. A t	9. A d
10. C d	10. B case	10. E √
11. E √	11. D //	11. D ww
12. A d	12. A case	12. D d
13. B t	13. D case	13. A case
14. D comp	14. A sp or d	14. B mm
15. C case	15. C //	15. B pref
16. D pref	16. D case	16. C comp
17. D d	17. A d	17. A pref
18. E √	18. C pref	18. C //

Sentence Error Answers X - XII

Sentence Errors X	Sentence Errors XI	Sentence Errors XII
1. B d	1. D pref	1. A ww
2. C s/v	2. D comp	2. A case
3. B case	3. B case	3. A t
4. D case	4. C case	4. B d
5. A d	5. B s/v	5. A d
6. E √	6. E √	6. C d
7. A d	7. E √	7. C pref
8. B nn	8. B d	8. C d
9. C pref	9. E √	9. C d
10. B d	10. D d	10. B case
11. E √	11. B d	11. A s/v
12. A case	12. C d	12. C pref
13. B d	13. A pref	13. B //
14. E √	14. E √	14. C comp
15. B pref	15. A pref	15. C d
16. C frag	16. B g	16. E √
17. C nn	17. C d	17. A d
18. E √	18. B d	18. D d

Improving Sentences

Select the letter of the best sentence correction, <u>if any is needed</u>, and place next to it the corresponding correction symbol. The first selection A duplicates the item.

Improving Sentences I

1. Erin Brokovich, an important fact-finder in prosecuting a Californian company for <u>pollution, she also is</u> the focus of a movie named after her.

    (A) pollution, she also is
    (B) pollution, which also is
    (C) pollution, is
    (D) pollution, since
    (E) pollution and thus is

2. <u>He took his dog</u> for a walk, my neighbor washed it.

    (A) He took his dog
    (B) The dog, having been taken
    (C) The dog was taken
    (D) He, taking his dog,
    (E) After he took his dog

3. Only since the Declaration of Independence <u>the United States have been considered</u> an independent nation.

    (A) the United States have been considered
    (B) the United states has been considered
    (C) have the United States considered being
    (D) were the United States considered being
    (E) was the United States considered

4. <u>To compare computers, technicians use terms like "gigahertz," being the speed that the clock inside the processor oscillates.</u>

    (A) To compare computers, technicians use terms like "gigahertz," being the speed that the clock inside the processor oscillates.
    (B) To compare computers, technicians use terms like "gigahertz," being the speed that the clock inside the processor oscillates.
    (C) To compare computers, technicians use terms like "gigahertz," which is the speed at which the clock inside the processor oscillates.
    (D) To compare computers, technicians use terms such as "gigahertz" which happens to be a term for the speed at which the clock within the processor is oscillating.
    (E) In the comparing of computers, technicians use "gigahertz" which describes the speed at which a processor's clock oscillates.

5. Although I do not get out of work until 6 P.M., <u>not being allowed to stay out no later than 9 P.M.</u>

    (A) not being allowed to stay out no later than 9 PM
    (B) I am not allowed to stay out past 9 P.M.
    (C) not being allowed to stay out past 9 P.M.
    (D) I can stay out no later past 9 P.M.
    (E) I don't stay out past 9 P.M.

6. The band had just begun to play and that was when the amplifier exploded, ending the show.

   (A) and that was when
   (B) after which thing had happened
   (C) until
   (D) when
   (E) because

7. Forever cemented in the minds of Americans, September 11th serves as a sobering example of our collective vulnerability to terrorism.

   (A) Forever cemented in the minds of Americans, September 11th serves as a sobering example of our collective vulnerability to terrorism.
   (B) Forever cemented in the minds of Americans, our collective vulnerability to terrorism was cemented by September 11th.
   (C) On September 11th our collective vulnerability to terrorism was cemented with a sobering attack forever.
   (D) The attacks of September 11th forever cement our minds with vulnerability to terrorism.
   (E) September 11th serves as a sobering example of our collective vulnerability to terrorism which cemented this in our mind.

8. Frantic over the loss of her iPod, Erin's search for it was desperately.

   (A) Erin's search for it was desperately.
   (B) Erin searched desperately for it.
   (C) Erin's search for it was desperate.
   (D) the search for it was desperate by Erin.
   (E) the iPod Erin searched for desperately.

9. Ray, Charlie, and Steven were driving when, swerving off the road, he crashed his car.

   (A) when, swerving off the road, he crashed his car.
   (B) and then he crashed his car after swerving off the road.
   (C) when Steven crashed his car after swerving off the road
   (D) when Steven crashed his car, since he swerved off the road.
   (E) and since Steve had swerved, he crashed his car.

10. The United States invaded Iraq believing that there were WMDs, but after the invasion, US officials determined that there were no WMDs in Iraq, this was the argument from the opposition to the war.

    (A) this was the argument from the opposition to the war.
    (B) which the opposition argued against the war.
    (C) the very argument those who were in opposition to the war supported.
    (D) it was the argument from the opposition to the war.
    (E) for the opposition to the war had argued.

11. A good leader not only exhibits good decision making but it commands a strong presence.

    (A) but it commands
    (B) which
    (C) but also commanding
    (D) but also commands
    (E) in addition to

12. Biological research often requires testing <u>where they</u> experiment on animals in order to determine the analogous response in humans.

    (A) where they
    (B) in which they
    (C) and the biologists
    (D) during which they
    (E) during which the biologists

13. I would prefer to marry <u>no one more than I would her.</u>

    (A) no one more than I would her.
    (B) no one more than she does.
    (C) no one rather than to marry her.
    (D) anyone rather than her.
    (E) her more than anyone.

14. <u>With a plethora of sources</u> for my research paper still to be found, my teacher tells me that I should continue finding sources before writing a draft.

    (A) With a plethora of sources
    (B) Because there is a plethora of sources
    (C) Because of a plethora of sources
    (D) By considering that there is the plethora of sources
    (E) Aware that there exists a plethora of sources

15. Many of my favorite possessions, such as my night light and my teddy bear, <u>coming from</u> my childhood.

    (A) coming from
    (B) they come from
    (C) they have come from
    (D) come from
    (E) which came from

16. <u>As students, the faculty believes that you</u> should attend classes regularly.

    (A) As students, the faculty believes that you
    (B) The belief of the faculty about students is that you
    (C) You, as students, are believed by the faculty, and you
    (D) The faculty, who believe that you, as students,
    (E) The faculty believes that as students, you

17. Discussing how to stay up-to-date on current affairs, <u>read the newspaper was my father's advice.</u>

    (A) read the newspaper was my father's advice
    (B) to read the newspaper was my father's advice
    (C) I was told by my father that his advice is read the newspaper
    (D) my father told me his advice is that reading the newspaper is a good way to stay up-to-date
    (E) my father advised me to read the newspaper.

18. The tour of the chocolate factory <u>begins with Willy Wonka greeting the children at the gate and culminates</u> with Wonka's handing over the factory to Charlie.

    (A) begins with Willy Wonka greeting the children at the gate and culminates
    (B) beginning with Willy Wonka greeting the children at the gate and culminating
    (C) that begins with Willy Wonka greeting the children at the gate and culminates
    (D) is begun with Willy Wonka greeting the children at the gate and culminated
    (E) begins with Willy Wonka's greeting the children at the gate and culminates

19. I was unable to reach the highest cabinet in our kitchen until I am twelve years old.

    (A) until I am twelve years old.
    (B) when I am twelve years old.
    (C) because I am twelve years old.
    (D) until I was twelve years old.
    (E) as I was twelve years old.

20. Laser printers are faster, better quality, and more reliable than ink jet printers, but the greater is its cost in total money.

    (A) the greater is its cost in total money.
    (B) they cost more.
    (C) in money the total cost is greater.
    (D) they cost greater in total money.
    (E) there is a greater cost in money.

21. Invaluable to their research, scientists rely on their machines to be calibrated accurately.

    (A) Invaluable to their research, scientists rely on their machines to be calibrated accurately.
    (B) Scientists, invaluable to their research, rely on their machines to be calibrated accurately
    (C) Invaluable to their research, scientists rely on their machines to be calibrated accurate.
    (D) Scientists rely on their machines, which are invaluable to their research, to be calibrated accurately.
    (E) It is invaluable to their research that scientists rely on their machines to be calibrated accurately.

22. Evidence quoted in my magazine and my favorite news programs show people taller than six feet tend to be more successful than people that are less than six feet tall.

    (A) show people taller than six feet tend to be
    (B) shows people taller than six feet tends to be
    (C) shows people taller than six feet tend to be
    (D) show that taller than six feet people tend to be
    (E) shows that taller than six feet people tends to be

23. Singing in the rural church choir their entire lives, Mark and Eric aspired to become singing duos in the big city some day.

    (A) to become singing duos
    (B) becoming singing duos
    (C) becoming a singing duo
    (D) of becoming singing duos
    (E) to become a singing duo

24. Before going to bed at night, my sister takes a shower, my brother reads a book first.

    (A) Before going to bed at night, my sister takes a shower, my brother reads a book first.
    (B) Before she goes to bed at night, my sister takes a shower and my brother reads a book.
    (C) Before my sister goes to bed, she takes a shower at night and my brother first reads a book.
    (D) Before my sister goes to bed at night, she takes a shower, whereas my brother reads a book before going to bed.
    (E) Before going to bed, at night, first taking a shower my sister, whereas first reading a book my brother.

25. Despite winning its final three games, the soccer team failed to qualify for the post season because of its previous losing streak.

(A) because of its previous losing streak.
(B) because previously it had been on a losing streak.
(C) because, in the past, many losses had been attained by them.
(D) because, having lost in the past, so they created a streak.
(E) since their losses were in a streak before.

Improving Sentences II

1. Last Sunday, more people from Maine visited the beaches in Massachusetts than New Hampshire.

    (A) New Hampshire
    (B) New Hampshire did
    (C) compared to New Hampshire's
    (D) New Hampshires's ones
    (E) in New Hampshire

2. Lucasfilm, Ltd, the company that pioneered special effects for *Star Wars, they also create* effects for many other full length feature movies.

    (A) "Star Wars", they also create
    (B) "Star Wars", also creating
    (C) "Star Wars", which also creates
    (D) "Star Wars", also creates
    (E) "Star Wars" and also creating

3. The office air conditioner is not as high powered as is my home.

    (A) as is my home.
    (B) as my home is.
    (C) as is my home's.
    (D) as is mine in the home.
    (E) as the one my home is having.

4. That you do that thing with your hair annoys me to no end.

    (A) That you do that thing with your hair annoys me
    (B) You doing that thing with your hair is annoying me
    (C) To do that thing which you are doing to your hair, is annoying me
    (D) I hate when you do that thing, which annoys me, with your hair
    (E) It is so annoying to me when with your hair you are doing that

5. The main functions of my Swiss army knife is cutting branches, whittling sticks, and to open up cans.

    (A) is cutting branches, whittling sticks, and to open up cans.
    (B) is to cut branches, to whittle sticks, and to open up cans.
    (C) are cutting branches, whittling sticks, and to open up cans.
    (D) is cutting branches, whittling sticks, and opening up cans.
    (E) are to cut branches, to whittle sticks, and to open up cans.

6. Joan and Mary hope to grow up and become a police officer.

    (A) to grow up and become a police officer.
    (B) growing up to become a police officer.
    (C) to grow up and to become a police officer.
    (D) to become police officers when they grow up.
    (E) growing up to become police officers

7. Cathy would like to go to the ball game, but the ball game is unable to be afforded by her.

    (A) Cathy would like to go to the ball game, but the ball game is unable to be afforded by her.
    (B) Cathy would like to go to the ball game, but she cannot afford to.
    (C) Cathy would like to go to the ball game, but she is unable to afford that.
    (D) The ball game is what Cathy would like to go to, but she cannot afford it.
    (E) The ball game appeals to Cathy, but she cannot afford going to it.

8. Like many new prisoners, the jail's rules were unfamiliar to Michael George.

   (A) the jail's rules were unfamiliar to Michael George.
   (B) the rules of the jail were unfamiliar to Michael George.
   (C) Michael George found the rules unfamiliar.
   (D) unfamiliar was what Michael George found the rules to be.
   (E) the jail's rules were found to be unfamiliar by Michael George.

9. Bill Gates, the CEO and founder of Microsoft, and who is the richest man in the world, donated money to provide AIDS vaccinations to Africans.

   (A) the CEO and founder of Microsoft, and who is the richest man in the world,
   (B) the CEO and founder of Microsoft, that is the richest man in the world,
   (C) Microsoft's CEO and founder, who is the richest man in the world,
   (D) who is the CEO and founder of Microsoft and the richest man in the world,
   (E) the Microsoft CEO and founder, who is also the richest man in the world

10. Before writing their reports, research must be conducted by students.

    (A) their reports, research must be conducted by students.
    (B) their reports, the students must conduct research.
    (C) their reports research must be conducted by the students
    (D) the reports of them, the students must have conducted research
    (E) the reports of them, the students must conduct research.

11. Although its being true, I still don't believe it.

    (A) Although its being true, I still don't believe it.
    (B) Despite its being true, I am not able to believe it.
    (C) Although it is of the state of being true, I still am not of the state of being able to believe it.
    (D) I don't believe it, even though it is true.
    (E) Although its true, I still don't believe it.

12. There is a basic difference between swords or daggers.

    (A) between swords or daggers.
    (B) between swords and daggers.
    (C) of swords and of daggers.
    (D) the swords and daggers are able of having.
    (E) belonging to the swords and daggers.

13. Living at sea no longer means to pack and unpack for each cruise.

    (A) no longer means to pack and unpack for each cruise.
    (B) thusly making packing and unpacking for each cruise unnecessary.
    (C) no longer means having packing and unpacking for each cruise.
    (D) no longer means packing and unpacking for each cruise.
    (E) means that no longer packing and unpacking for each cruise is necessary.

14. Anyone who knows the Ted Williams story knows where they were when he hit over .400 for his final time.

    (A) Anyone who knows the Ted Williams story knows where they were when he
    (B) Anyone who knows of Ted William's story knows where they were when he
    (C) Anybody who knows of the Ted Williams story knows where he was when he
    (D) Anyone who knows the Ted Williams story knows where he or she was when Ted Williams
    (E) Anyone who knows of Ted Williams and his story knows where they were when Ted Williams.

15. The traveling salesman came this far, he wanted to sell us premium-quality vacuum cleaners.

    (A) The traveling salesmen came this far, he
    (B) Coming this far the traveling salesman, he
    (C) Having come this far, the traveling salesman
    (D) As the traveling salesman came this far,
    (E) Since coming thus far, he

16. Our teacher gave us our assignment, and we split into groups, and we started working, continuing to do so for the remainder of the period.

    (A) and we split into groups, and we started working, continuing to do so
    (B) and we split into groups, started working, and continuing to do so
    (C) and we split into groups, started working, and continued to do so
    (D) and we split into groups. We started working and continuing to do so
    (E) and we split into groups, starting to work, continuing to do so

17. Before Keleigh was allowed to leave the tutor's office, she had to finish her work, receive her homework assignment, and she had to call her mother in to have a conference with Mr. Beaven.

    (A) she had to finish her work, receive her homework assignment, and she had to call her mother
    (B) she had to finish her work, receiving her homework assignment, and she had to call her mother.
    (C) she had to finish her work and receive her homework assignment, then she had to call her mother
    (D) finishing her work and receiving her homework assignment, she had to call her mother
    (E) she had to finish her work, receive her homework assignment, and call her mother

18. Recruiting talented athletes from the Midwest is usually not as easy as it is in the Northeast, where there are many more people who are better at sports.

    (A) as it is in the Northeast, where there are
    (B) as, being in the Northeast, there are
    (C) as, where there are more in the Northeast, so
    (D) as it is in that of the Northeast, where there are
    (E) as in the Northeast, where there are

19. The girl would be attractive if she wasn't wearing so much makeup.

    (A) if she wasn't wearing so much makeup.
    (B) if she weren't wearing so much makeup.
    (C) if less makeup she had on her.
    (D) wearing less makeup on her.
    (E) had she not worn so much of makeup.

20. The building was as pretty as if painted by angels.

    (A) as pretty as if painted by angels.
    (B) pretty, as if painted by angels.
    (C) as pretty as if angels had painted it.
    (D) pretty as if angels had painted it.
    (E) pretty, as if angels having painted it.

21. Inflating gas prices, having rose by 100% in the last two years, threatens to harm the economy in the foreseeable future

    (A) having rose by 100% in the last two years, threatens
    (B) having rose by 100% in the last two years, threaten
    (C) have rose by 100% in the last two years, threatens
    (D) have risen by 100% in the last two years, threatening
    (E) having risen by 100% in the last two years, now threaten

22. Do not break the mirror, you will slice your wrists and you will have seven years of bad luck.

    (A) mirror, you will slice your wrists and you will have
    (B) mirror; you will slice your wrists and have
    (C) mirror; you will slice your wrists and then will have
    (D) mirror, there is a possibility of your slicing your wrists and accruing
    (E) mirror, risking to slice your wrists and to have

23. Today the main function of pagers is to alert doctors when there is an emergency, whereas before as everyone used them as a personal communications device.

    (A) there is an emergency, whereas before as everyone used them
    (B) there is an emergency, where as before, everyone was using them
    (C) there is an emergency, whereas before everyone used them
    (D) there becomes an emergency, whereas before having used them
    (E) there becomes an emergency, where as everyone before was using them

24. The Bush administration, often by covert or undisclosed means, tried to impose their philosophy on the Middle-East by sending in troops to raid Iraqi villages.

    (A) tried to impose their philosophy on the Middle-East by sending in troops
    (B) trying to impose their philosophy on the Middle-East and sending in troops
    (C) tried imposing their philosophy on the Middle-East by sending in troops
    (D) tried to impose its philosophy on the Middle-East by sending in troops
    (E) tried to impose its philosophy on the Middle-East in having sent troops

25. The ozone layer, which protects us from harmful UV rays, it is slowly deteriorating.

    (A) which protects us from harmful UV rays, it is slowly deteriorating.
    (B) protecting us from harmful UV rays, is slowly deteriorating.
    (C) which protects us from harmful UV rays, is slowly deteriorating.
    (D) having protected us from harmful UV rays, not it is slowly deteriorating.
    (E) who protects us from harmful UV rays, now is slowly deteriorating.

Improving Sentences III

1. Apparently dissatisfied by their first race, the crew team members <u>hope attempting</u> a second time so that they may atone for their poor performance.

   (A) hopes attempting
   (B) hope to attempt
   (C) hopes it can
   (D) have hopes to attempt
   (E) are having hopes of attempting

2. Bill Gates, a dropout from Harvard in the 1970s, <u>and eventually to form and run his own company, Microsoft.</u>

   (A) and eventually to form and run his own company, Microsoft.
   (B) eventually formed and ran his own company, Microsoft.
   (C) and eventually to form and to run his own company, Microsoft.
   (D) eventually had his own company, Microsoft, that he formed and ran.
   (E) eventually forming and running his own company, Microsoft.

3. Lying cannot be compared equally to fibbing, <u>for lying is harmful, whereas fibbing is not.</u>

   (A) for lying is harmful, whereas fibbing is not.
   (B) since it is harmful to lie but fibbing is not.
   (C) because it is harmful
   (D) because the two differ regarding harmfulness
   (E) because of its harmful nature

4. A president should provide forceful leadership <u>but with their goal to be</u> a balanced, representative executive.

   (A) but with their goal to be
   (B) but with his goal to be
   (C) but also trying to be
   (D) but should also be
   (E) but they should be

5. The children won their baseball <u>game, played</u> good defense, including Michael's diving catch during the fourth inning.

   (A) game, played
   (B) game playing
   (C) game; and played
   (D) game by playing
   (E) game with the playing of

6. The captain of the ship pointed <u>to the roughness of the water as harsh and choppy.</u>

   (A) to the roughness of the water as harsh and choppy.
   (B) to the harsh and choppy water, being rough.
   (C) out that the water was harsh and choppy.
   (D) the harsh and choppy roughness of the water.
   (E) how the water was harsh and choppy and rough.

7. Greg was not only a great swimmer but also <u>he was a terrific cyclist.</u>

   (A) he was a terrific cyclist.
   (B) having been a terrific cyclist.
   (C) being a terrific cyclist
   (D) cycling terrifically
   (E) a terrific cyclist

8. <u>Although, in my opinion, green grapes from the vine are tastier than red grapes, my brother prefers red ones.</u>

   (A) Although, in my opinion, green grapes from the vine are tastier than red grapes, my brother prefers red ones.
   (B) Although my brother prefers red grapes, green grapes from the vine are tastier.
   (C) I prefer green grapes, my brother prefers red grapes.
   (D) Green vine grapes are tastier than red grapes so my brother prefers red grapes.
   (E) Since I think green grapes are tastier than red grapes, my brother prefers red ones.

9. Because I wore sunscreen with a high SPF when I went to the beach, this protected me from getting a sunburn.

    (A) this protected me from getting a sunburn.
    (B) I did not get a sunburn.
    (C) and it protected me from getting a sunburn.
    (D) this protected me from getting sunburned.
    (E) so I was protected without a sunburn.

10. Lacking the proper tools, the table which I made did not come out level.

    (A) Lacking the proper tools, the table which I made did not come out level.
    (B) Lacking the proper tools, the table that I made did not come out level.
    (C) Lacking the proper tools, I made a table which was not level.
    (D) The unlevel table was made by my lacking tools.
    (E) Because I lacked the proper tools, I did not make a level table.

11. I was up so late last night and thus am extremely tired today.

    (A) so late last night and thus
    (B) so late last night that I
    (C) late last night and therefore
    (D) late at such an hour that I
    (E) late, and so I

12. By eating healthily and exercising often, a fit body can be achieved and maintained by nearly anyone.

    (A) a fit body can be achieved and maintained by nearly anyone.
    (B) nearly anyone is able to achieve and maintain a fit body.
    (C) it is possible that nearly anyone may be as able to achieve a fit body and maintain it.
    (D) by achieving and maintaining a fit body for nearly anyone.
    (E) your body can be achieved and maintained to be fit.

13. Most scientists agree that life not only began as single-celled organisms but also it started off the African coast.

    (A) but also it started off the African coast.
    (B) but also it had started off the coast of Africa.
    (C) but also started off the African coast.
    (D) but also, off the coast of Africa, it started.
    (E) and started off the African coast.

14. After the three hour delay, the airport terminal was crowded with people who, although they were from diverse parts of the country and had never met, they all sensed a bond due to their delayed travel.

    (A) they all sensed a bond.
    (B) sense a bond
    (C) sensing a bond
    (D) might have sensed a bond
    (E) are sensing a bond

15. The Boy Scouts coming this far, did not want to turn back without reaching the top of the mountain.

    (A) The Boy Scouts coming this far
    (B) The Boy Scouts had come this far
    (C) Having come this far, the Boy Scouts
    (D) To come this far, the Boy Scouts
    (E) The Boy Scouts came so far, so that they

16. Upon returning home, Billy appeared as dirty as if rolling in the mud.

    (A) if rolling
    (B) having rolled
    (C) if from rolling
    (D) if he had rolled
    (E) if he would have rolled

17. The backgrounds of the London suicide bombers is increasingly well documented.

    (A) is increasingly well documented
    (B) is more and more documented
    (C) are increasingly well documented
    (D) are increasing in better documentation
    (E) has increased in better documentation

18. The subject the philosopher pondered, which was whether it is better to have loved and lost than to have never loved at all.

   (A) pondered, which was whether it is better to have loved and lost
   (B) pondered was if it would be better they would love and lose
   (C) pondered was that loving and losing would result better
   (D) pondered was will loving and losing mean more
   (E) pondered was whether it is better to have loved and to have lost

19. Gandhi, the most prominent leader of the non-violence movement, doing it despite harsh criticism from belligerent nations.

   (A) Gandhi, the most prominent leader of the non-violence movement, doing it
   (B) Gandhi the most prominent leader of the non-violence movement, and who did
   (C) Gandhi was the most prominent leader of the non-violence movement and led the movement
   (D) Gandhi was the most prominent leader of the non-violence movement
   (E) Gandhi, the most prominent leader of the non-violence movement had been leading the movement

20. As the temperature reached in excess of 100 degrees, the children were hesitant to play outside.

   (A) As the temperature reached in excess of 100 degrees
   (B) As the temperature peaked the excess of 100 degrees
   (C) When the degrees were over 100
   (D) After the degrees surpassed 100
   (E) The degrees, having surpassed an excess of 100

21. The Titanic, supposedly indestructible, crashed into an iceberg, and it was sunk.

   (A) an iceberg, and it was sunk.
   (B) an iceberg and sinking it.
   (C) an iceberg, with the result being it sank.
   (D) an iceberg so that it sank.
   (E) an iceberg and sank.

22. A victory in our soccer game last week would have ensured us going to the playoffs.

   (A) would have ensured us going to the playoffs.
   (B) would ensure us going to the playoffs.
   (C) had ensured us going to the playoffs.
   (D) would have ensured our going to the playoffs
   (E) was ensuring us going to the playoffs

23. The wretched schoolteacher believed that if you assign a lot of homework, students could learn more.

   (A) if you assign a lot of homework, students could
   (B) with assigning a lot of homework, students will
   (C) homework assigned to students makes them
   (D) by her assigning a lot of homework students could
   (E) assigning a lot of homework, students could

24. The witch is mean, and that is why she casts evil spells on little children.

   (A) The witch is mean, and that is why she casts evil spells on little children.
   (B) Because the witch is mean, and that is why she casts evil spells on little children.
   (C) The witch is mean, therefore she casts evil spells on little children.
   (D) Because the witch is mean, she casts evil spells on little children.
   (E) Because the witch casts evil spells on children whom are little, she is therefore mean.

25. It is common knowledge that smoking is bad for you, and the majority of the smoking population knows many methods how to quit <u>permanently and stay clean.</u>

   (A) permanently and staying clean.
   (B) permanent and stay clean
   (C) and to stay clean permanently
   (D) and to permanently stay clean
   (E) having permanently stayed clean

Improving Sentences IV

1. The Beatles <u>was so well known that even recluses were</u> aware of them.

   (A) was so well known that even recluses were
   (B) were so well known that even recluses was
   (C) were so well known that even recluses is
   (D) were so well known that even recluses would have to have been
   (E) were so well known that even recluses were

2. The tsunami was so violent that it destroyed buildings, ruined lives, and <u>people were killed.</u>

   (A) people were killed.
   (B) people were being killed
   (C) killed people
   (D) killing people
   (E) thusly killing people

3. As I worked diligently on an SAT, the girl next to me <u>is turning to me to ask</u> what the homework had been.

   (A) is turning to me to ask
   (B) turned to me and asked
   (C) turns to me and is asking
   (D) turns and also asks me
   (E) would turn and ask me

4. No one <u>is more stronger than me.</u>

   (A) is more stronger than me.
   (B) is stronger than me.
   (C) is more strong than I.
   (D) is more strong than I.
   (E) is stronger than I.

5. <u>The homework having been finished,</u> Jay went outside to play.

   (A) The homework having been finished
   (B) The homework being finished
   (C) The homework, when he finished it
   (D) When having finished the homework
   (E) When he finished his homework

6. <u>Whether George Bush actually won the 2000 election or did not in Florida</u> remains hotly contested, but nevertheless he is our current president

   (A) Whether George Bush actually won the 2000 election or did not in Florida
   (B) Whether or not George Bush actually won the 2000 election in Florida
   (C) In Florida, whether or not George Bush actually won the 2000 election
   (D) Whether or not George Bush actually won in Florida in the 2000 election
   (E) In the 2000 election, whether George Bush won Florida or not

7. <u>Neither Ron nor Harry was attracted to Hermione.</u>

   (A) Neither Ron nor Harry was attracted to Hermione.
   (B) Neither Ron or Harry was attracted to Hermione.
   (C) Ron nor Harry was neither attracted to Hermione.
   (D) Hermione was neither attractive to Ron nor Harry.
   (E) Ron and Harry were neither attracted to Hermione.

8. The enemy's base having been infiltrated, the soldiers began the onslaught.

   (A) The enemy's base having been infiltrated
   (B) The base of the enemy being infiltrated
   (C) At the base of the enemy, which they infiltrated
   (D) When they had infiltrated the enemy's base
   (E) When having infiltrated the enemy's base

9. Although criticized by many racists that opposed African-Americans' playing in the Major Leagues, most people viewed Jackie Robinson as a skillful player.

   (A) most people viewed Jackie Robinson as a skillful player.
   (B) most people viewed Jackie Robinson to be a skillful player.
   (C) a skillful player was what Jackie Robinson as.
   (D) Jackie Robinson was viewed by most people as a skillful player.
   (E) Jackie Robinson, a skillful player in the view of most people.

10. For as many as 86 years and more, the Boston Red Sox did not win a world championship

    (A) For as many as 86 years and more
    (B) For not much more than about 86 years
    (C) For a little over 86 years and more
    (D) For 86 years and then some
    (E) For more than 86 years

11. The intelligence of orangutans is often as sophisticated as a first-grader.

    (A) as a first-grader
    (B) as that of a first-grader
    (C) like a first-grader
    (D) such as a first-grader
    (E) like a first-grader's

12. Gustav, the champion alligator wrestler of Sweden, winning the championship by a unanimous decision.

    (A) Sweden, winning the championship by a unanimous decision.
    (B) Sweden, winning the championship, which was decided unanimously.
    (C) Sweden, and he won the championship by a unanimous decision.
    (D) Sweden, won the championship by a unanimous decision.
    (E) Sweden, a unanimous decision earning him a win in the championship.

13. Anyone who has high expectations of or is reasonably excited about tonight's lecture will not be disappointed.

    (A) has high expectations or is reasonably excited about
    (B) has high expectations or else excitement in reasonable amounts about
    (C) is highly expectant or who has reasonable excitement instead
    (D) is highly expectant or reasonable excitement about
    (E) has either expectations that are high or reasonable excitements

14. The more you use of expletives, the more our language will become vulgar and unsophisticated.

    (A) The more you use of expletives
    (B) The more we use of expletives
    (C) The more expletives are used
    (D) As the use of expletives increases
    (E) As you use more expletives

15. Having a Sherpa as their leader and a trusty map helped their navigation of the mountain.

    (A) Having a Sherpa as their leader and a trusty map helped
    (B) Having the leadership of a Sherpa and a trusty map helped
    (C) A Sherpa as their leader and a trusty map as their guide helped
    (D) To be led by a Sherpa and a trusty map helped
    (E) A Sherpa as their leader and a map to be trusted helped

16. The secretary was asked to verify the intern's documenting on last year's TPS Reports.

    (A) the intern's documenting
    (B) the document of an intern
    (C) the documenting of an intern
    (D) that intern who documented
    (E) the intern's documentation

17. Scientists argue that dinosaurs became extinct, the reason for this is possibly a meteor.

    (A) extinct, the reason for this is possibly a meteor.
    (B) extinct, the reason possibly being a meteor.
    (C) extinct; possibly by a meteor.
    (D) extinct due to a meteor.
    (E) extinct possibly due to a meteor.

18. My family is putting up fences, for it will deter animals.

    (A) fences, for it will deter
    (B) fences, in which it will deter
    (C) fences to deter
    (D) fences, for the deterrence of
    (E) fences, being able to deter

19. Critics of John Stewart say that his show is unwatchable for the reason that his reports were critical always of Republicans.

    (A) for the reason that his reports are critical always of Republicans.
    (B) since his reports for the Republicans are always critical.
    (C) because his criticism for the Republicans is always in his reports.
    (D) the fact being that his reports are always critical of the Republicans.
    (E) because his reports are always critical of the Republicans.

20. After determining the causes of the infection, I was able to cure the patient.

    (A) infection, I was able to cure the patient.
    (B) infection, and I was able to cure the patient.
    (C) infection, and I cured the patient.
    (D) infection that I cured the patient.
    (E) infection, which cured the patient.

21. Of all the teams in the league, the cleanup hitter from New Hampshire was clearly the strongest.

    (A) Of all the teams in the league, the cleanup hitter from New Hampshire was clearly the strongest.
    (B) Of all the teams in the league, the cleanup hitter from New Hampshire was the strongest.
    (C) New Hampshire's cleanup hitter was clearly the strongest player in the league.
    (D) New Hampshire, whose cleanup hitter was clearly the strongest player in the league.
    (E) Cleanup hitters, especially that of New Hampshire, are the strongest players in the league.

22. The guitar player was skilled, his fingers were quick.

   (A) The guitar player was skilled, his fingers were quick.
   (B) Because the guitar player was skilled, his fingers were quick.
   (C) The guitar player was skilled, whereas his fingers were quick.
   (D) The guitar player was skilled; his fingers were quick.
   (E) Despite being skilled, the guitar player's fingers were quick.

23. The anxious boy looked for a way to quickly pass the time before his date.

   (A) to quickly pass the time before his date.
   (B) to pass the time quickly before his date.
   (C) to pass the time before his quick date.
   (D) quickly to pass the time before his date.
   (E) so that he passed time quickly before his date.

24. During recess, the boy was playing football, swinging on the swing set, and won a relay race.

   (A) was playing football, swinging on the swing set, and won a relay race.
   (B) was playing football, swung on the swing set, and won a relay race.
   (C) played football, swinging on the swing set, and won a relay race.
   (D) had played football, swung, and winning a relay race.
   (E) was playing football, was swinging on the swing set, and was winning a relay race.

25. Having brang a snake to show and tell, the student was expelled.

   (A) Having brang a snake to show and tell,
   (B) Because he had brang a snake to show and tell,
   (C) For the reason of bringing a snake to show and tell,
   (D) Since bringing a snake to show and tell
   (E) Because he brought a snake to show and tell,

Improving Sentences V

1. Often encountering spiders in cobwebs found in her basement, <u>Kelly swatting them down so that they will be less quick to reproduce.</u>

   (A) Kelly swatting them down so that they will be less quick to reproduce.
   (B) Kelly has been swatting them down, in order to prevent their quick reproduction.
   (C) Kelly swats them down so that they cannot reproduce so quickly.
   (D) Kelly swats them down, being that their reproducing would not occur at such a quick rate.
   (E) Kelly having swatted them down so that they would not reproduce so quick.

2. Many children tried out for roles as extras in the Broadway production "Annie", <u>and only a few were selected.</u>

   (A) and only a few were selected.
   (B) but only a few were selected.
   (C) however only a few were selected.
   (D) inasmuch as only a few were selected.
   (E) being that only a few were selected.

3. The craftsman, skillfully scraping away at his wood block, <u>trying to fashion an intricate carving of his subject.</u>

   (A) trying to fashion an intricate carving of his subject.
   (B) has been trying to have fashioned an intricate carving of his subject.
   (C) had tried to be fashioning an intricate carving of his subject.
   (D) is trying, if not fashioning, an intricate carving of his subject.
   (E) is trying to fashion an intricate carving of his subject.

4. Picasso, <u>a famous artist of the Cubism style, whose works are world-renowned for their</u> symbolism and intricacy of detail.

   (A) a famous artist of the Cubism style, whose works are world-renowned for their
   (B) a famous artist of the Cubism style, his works are world-renowned for their
   (C) a famous artist of the Cubism style's works are world-renowned for their
   (D) famously an artist of the Cubism style, whose works are world-renowned for their
   (E) an artist famous for his work in the Cubism style, is world-renowned for his

5. Many alterations needed to be made to the dress, <u>and they increased its length as well as waist.</u>

   (A) and they increased its length as well as waist.
   (B) increasing its length as well as its waist.
   (C) requiring increased length as well as waist.
   (D) including increases in length and waist.
   (E) needing an increase in length and also an increase in waist.

6. <u>Although America's cars are known for their inferiority to Japan's long-lasting, fuel-efficient vehicles, Japan</u> may start to produce the same quality as America.

   (A) Although America's cars are known for their inferiority to Japan's long-lasting, fuel-efficient vehicles, Japan
   (B) Although America is known for producing cars that are inferior to those of Japan, Japan
   (C) Being that America's cars are known for being inferior to Japan's long- lasting, fuel-efficient vehicles, Japan
   (D) Although America is know for its production of cars that are inferior to Japan's, they
   (E) Because America's cars are known for their inferiority to Japan's, so they

7. Stem-cell research and organ cloning have proven to be able to help many disease victims, <u>this being the reason that its R&D continues to be appointed by Bush.</u>

   (A) this being the reason that its R&D continues to be appointed by Bush.
   (B) and, as a result, Bush continues to invest money in R&D.
   (C) and that is exactly why R&D continues to be appointed by Bush.
   (D) showing the reasons why R&D is continuing to be appointed by Bush.
   (E) and the reason that R&D continues to have money invested in it by Bush is this.

8. Emeril Lagasse, <u>who is a nationally-televised chef with his own show, and is making</u> over $12 million a year.

   (A) who is a nationally-televised chef with his own show, and is making
   (B) being a nationally-televised chef and having his own show, who is making
   (C) a nationally-televised chef with his own show, makes
   (D) a nationally-televised chef having his own show, makes
   (E) who, being nationally televised with his own show, makes

9. <u>While reading his brand new Harry Potter novel, that was when Jimmy</u> wanted to become an author.

   (A) While reading his brand new Harry Potter novel, that was when Jimmy
   (B) While reading his brand new Harry Potter novel, Jimmy decided then that he
   (C) While Jimmy was reading his brand new Harry Potter novel, he was deciding that he
   (D) When Jimmy was reading his brand new Harry Potter novel, it was when he
   (E) Jimmy, having read his brand new Harry Potter novel, decided he

10. Bruce Wayne decided to take the "Batmobile" out for a <u>drive, and he would pick up some groceries.</u>

    (A) drive, and he would pick up some groceries.
    (B) drive, picking up some groceries.
    (C) drive, and then he would pick up some groceries.
    (D) drive to pick up groceries.
    (E) drive, and then would pick up groceries.

11. It is believed that the ancient Egyptians used poison ivy to deter potential looters from attempting to rob their tombs.

    (A) used poison ivy to deter potential looters from attempting to rob
    (B) were using poison ivy to assist in deterring potential looters from robbing
    (C) used poison ivy to deter potential looters from having attempted to be robbing
    (D) were using poison ivy to assist them in deterring potential looters from attempting to rob
    (E) using poison ivy, deterring potential looters, and from attempting to rob

12. It seems that one of the most sought after Picasso prints are not being reproduced because of a flaw in copyright law.

    (A) are not being reproduced because of
    (B) are never going to be reproduced seeing that
    (C) is not being reproduced because of
    (D) is not going to be reproduced seeing that there is
    (E) are never going to be reproduced because of

13. The students believed that at the end of the year they would have less work, but actually they had more work to do in the beginning.

    (A) but actually they had more work to do in the beginning.
    (B) actually they had more work to do in the beginning.
    (C) and in fact they did work more in the beginning.
    (D) but having worked more in the beginning, they did so more.
    (E) but they did so more than in the beginning.

14. Bill prefers Boston sports teams than of New York and California.

    (A) than of New York and California.
    (B) rather than those of New York and California.
    (C) to those of New York and California.
    (D) than of the teams being from New York and California.
    (E) more than New York and California.

15. Although a licensed doctor, Mr. Smith chose not to pursue a career in the medical field.

    (A) Although a licensed doctor, Mr. Smith chose not to pursue
    (B) Although he having been licensed as a doctor, Mr. Smith chose not to pursue
    (C) Even though him being a licensed doctor, Mr. Smith chose to not pursue
    (D) Although he was having been licensed as a doctor, Mr. Smith chose to not pursue
    (E) Even as a licensed doctor, Mr. Smith is not pursuing

16. Kay got a better grade than either Sue or Cathy.

    (A) than either Sue or Cathy.
    (B) than either Sue or Cathy did.
    (C) than either did Sue, or did Cathy.
    (D) than did Sue or Cathy either.
    (E) that was superior to that of Cathy or Sue.

17. Because of Mongolian rats were the cause of many problems, Europe sought ways to end their infestation.

(A) Because of Mongolian rats were the cause of many problems,
(B) Because Mongolian rats were the cause of many problems,
(C) Because of Mongolian rats were the cause of many problems,
(D) Mongolian rats were causing many problems,
(E) Mongolian rats were the cause of many problems, and because of that

18. Since minks are only found in select area's, their pelts are very valuable.

(A) Since minks are only found in select area's,
(B) Since minks is only found in select area's,
(C) Since minks are found only in select areas,
(D) Being that minks are found only in select areas,
(E) Despite minks being found only in select areas,

19. The pirates pillaged the village and are seeking buried treasure.

(A) The pirates pillaged the village and are seeking buried treasure.
(B) The pirates pillaged the village and seeked out buried treasure.
(C) The pirates having pillaged the village and will be seeking buried treasure.
(D) The pirates pillaged the village and sought buried treasure.
(E) The pirates, having sought buried treasure, pillaged the village.

20. Fred feared heights, bugs and watching horror movies, but his greatest dread was taking finals, which came every June.

(A) heights, bugs and watching horror movies, but
(B) heights and bugs, and watching horror movies, but
(C) heights, bugs, and horror movies, but
(D) heights, and bugs and watching movies of horror, yet
(E) heights, bugs and watching horror movies, and

21. The book explains how one of the soldiers worked on would be doing after the war.

(A) one of the soldiers worked on would be doing after the war.
(B) one of the soldiers, working would be doing after the war.
(C) one of the soldiers, having worked, would be doing after the war.
(D) one of the soldiers had worked after the war.
(E) that one of the soldiers had been working after the war.

22. This summer Timothy hopes to learn many new things about geometry and algebra, both of which will be taken next year.

(A) both of which will be taken next year.
(B) both of which he will be taking next year.
(C) both of which will be taken by him next year.
(D) which both are being taken next year by him.
(E) which he will take both next year.

23. The biggest game of the season, played between the Red Sox and the <u>Yankees, was held at Fenway Park in Boston.</u>

   (A) Yankees, was held at Fenway Park in Boston.
   (B) Yankees and was held at Fenway Park in Boston.
   (C) Yankees was held at Fenway Park in Boston.
   (D) Yankees, being held at Fenway Park in Boston.
   (E) Yankees, was being held at Fenway Park in Boston.

24. Timmy picked Jimmy up at 8:30, <u>and by then after a shower Jimmy was almost fully awake.</u>

   (A) and by then after a shower Jimmy was almost fully awake.
   (B) and by then, after having took a shower, Jimmy was almost fully awake.
   (C) by then Jimmy was almost fully awake after a shower.
   (D) and had by then taken a shower Jimmy was almost fully awake.
   (E) and by then, after having taken a shower, Jimmy was almost fully awake.

25. The girl meant the world to <u>him, he was her best friend.</u>

   (A) him, he was her best friend.
   (B) him, being that she was his best friend.
   (C) him, seeing as she was his best friend.
   (D) him; she was his best friend.
   (E) him; that she was his best friend.

Improving Sentences VI

1. Having Bill Gates as its CEO <u>and a programming team with a keen sense of software helped to establish</u> Microsoft as the world's most successful corporation.

   (A) and a programming team with a keen sense of software helped to establish
   (B) and a team for programming with a keen sense of software helped establish
   (C) and a programming team as a key tool in producing good software helped to establish
   (D) and a team of programmers, being that their sense of software was keen, so it helped to make
   (E) and a team who could program with a keen sense of software helped to establish

2. Do not allow pets in the apartment complex, <u>they could dirty the rugs.</u>

   (A) they could dirty the rugs.
   (B) for they might dirty the rugs.
   (C) the rugs could be dirtied by them.
   (D) they might have dirtied the rugs.
   (E) who could dirty the rugs.

3. Although respected by some students as a knowledgeable teacher, <u>Dr. Haggard was thought of by most of his colleagues</u> as a fake.

   (A) Dr. Haggard was thought of by most of his colleagues
   (B) most his colleagues thought of him
   (C) it seemed Dr. Haggard
   (D) Dr. Haggard, most of his colleagues said, was
   (E) it was thought by many of his colleagues that Dr. Haggard was more

4. The Legal Seafood chain began with a small restaurant in Boston, <u>and there were no more built until</u> ten years after that one was erected.

   (A) and there were no more built until
   (B) and nobody built another one until
   (C) but another one was not built for
   (D) it stood alone until
   (E) another one of which was not built until

5. <u>People that might be considered a threat to society because they have committed</u> serious crimes are tried and, after a just trial, sent to prison.

   (A) People that might be considered a threat to society because they have committed
   (B) People possibly being considered threats to society because they have committed
   (C) People who are threatening society because of committing
   (D) People who might be considered threatening to society because of committing
   (E) In the past, if people whom are threatening because of committing

6. Even though James loves computers, he does not own one of his own, <u>nor does any member of his family.</u>
   (A) nor does any member of his family
   (B) and neither do any of his family members.
   (C) and nor does any of his family.
   (D) neither do any of his family members.
   (E) and his family do not either.

7. As I whispered to my brother the name of the girl I liked, <u>a windstorm is howling so that</u> he could not hear what I had to say.

   (A) a windstorm is howling so that
   (B) a windstorm howled so as to make it so that
   (C) a windstorm howled so that
   (D) the howling of a windstorm was making it so that
   (E) over the howling of a windstorm

8. The Red Sox won the World Series in 1918, even so, not winning again until 2004.

   (A) even so, not winning again until
   (B) not having had a win again until
   (C) yet without winning another until
   (D) and they didn't win again until
   (E) but they did not win again until

9. The computer game having crashed in a matter of two hours, my brother brought it back to the store and demanded a refund.

   (A) The computer game having crashed in a matter of two hours,
   (B) It crashed after only two house, and
   (C) The computer game took only two hours to crash, and
   (D) Taking only two hours to be crashed,
   (E) The computer game, crashing in only two hours,

10. One of the most versatile and heavy duty new kitchen tools were available for so little money that consumers became skeptical of its quality.

    (A) kitchen tools were available for so little money that
    (B) kitchen tools was available for so little money that
    (C) tools for the kitchen were, for so little money, available, and
    (D) kitchen tools was available, costing so little money that
    (E) kitchen tools, costing so little money that

11. Of all of the people representing the different colleges at the fair, only Princeton was informative, patient, and nice.

    (A) only Princeton was
    (B) it was only Princeton who were
    (C) only the representative of Princeton was
    (D) only that individual whose occupation it was to represent Princeton was
    (E) only at Princeton were

12. A news reporter was sent last night to film a New Hampshire resident's eye-witness encounter, he had witnessed the theft of Mr. D'Angelo's Ferrari.

    (A) encounter, he had witnessed the theft of
    (B) encounter, having had witnessed the theft of
    (C) depiction of the witnessing of the unknown thief's stealing
    (D) encounter, but instead he witnessed
    (E) encounter of the theft of

13. Many teachers are starting their own fun after-school programs, for it will encourage students to view school in a positive light.

    (A) for it will encourage students to view school
    (B) for students will be encouraged thus to view school
    (C) hopefully encouraging students to view school
    (D) in the hope of encouraging students to view school
    (E) hoping to encourage the students' viewing of school

14. Miles Davis, one of the country's leading jazz musicians, having performed at least once in every state across the country.

    (A) having performed at least once in every state
    (B) has been performing at least once in every state
    (C) has performed at least once in every state
    (D) being a performer, has done so at least once in every state
    (E) has done a performance, once in every state, at least,

15. The more you hear classical music, the more our brains will come to appreciate its natural lightness and profundity.

    (A) the more our brains will come to appreciate
    (B) the more your brain will come to appreciate
    (C) the more it will become that our brains can appreciate
    (D) the more we can develop an appreciation for
    (E) the more it becomes clear that our brains must appreciate

16. One pursuing a degree in law and business could spend as many as eight years or more in undergraduate and professional school.

    (A) as many as eight years or more
    (B) many, possibly eight years or more
    (C) a great many years – eight or more being
    (D) eight years or more
    (E) more than, or at least as many as eight years

17. The movie production crew moved into New York to film, disrupting businesses, closing streets, and many fans came to watch the filming.

    (A) and many fans came to watch the filming
    (B) and many fans coming to watch the filming.
    (C) and the filming brought many fans to watch.
    (D) and attracting many fans to watch the filming.
    (E) and having attracted many fans to watch the filming.

18. Shattered in an instant by a mallet, the vase had stood on the mantle for over fifteen years.

    (A) the vase had stood on the mantle for over fifteen years.
    (B) the vase was standing on the mantle for over fifteen years.
    (C) for fifteen years had that vase been standing on the mantle.
    (D) that vase stood over fifteen years on the mantle.
    (E) for fifteen years had that vase having stood on the mantle.

19. Nobody is more happier for you than me that you were able to attend my party.

    (A) more happier for you than me
    (B) more happy for you than me
    (C) happier for you than me
    (D) happier for you than I
    (E) more happier for you than I

20. Whether you imbibed enough alcohol to legally intoxicate yourself that night or did not, you should not have been drinking while you were pregnant.

    (A) Whether you imbibed enough alcohol to legally intoxicate yourself that night or did not,
    (B) Whether or not you imbibed enough alcohol to legally intoxicate yourself that night,
    (C) Whether it was the case or not that that night you had imbibed an amount of alcohol sufficient to intoxicate yourself legally,
    (D) Independent of the case that you imbibed the alcohol necessary to intoxicate yourself, or did not,
    (E) Having imbibed enough alcohol to intoxicate yourself legally, or not as well,

21. My parents did not think it was wise to leave deciding about his summer activities to Dan without any of their input.

   (A) deciding about his summer activities to Dan without any of their input.
   (B) Dan to deciding about his summer activities without their being able to put any of theirs in.
   (C) Dan to decide on his own what he should be doing with his summer.
   (D) the deciding on summer activities for Dan to himself.
   (E) Dan to decide about what the activities of his summer were going to be by himself.

22. Anyone who has agility or is reasonably quick can pick up basic gymnastics easily.

   (A) or is reasonably quick
   (B) or acts reasonably quickly
   (C) can be reasonable and quick
   (D) is quickly reasonable
   (E) or reasonable quickness

23. The vacation hours of a restaurant waiter are often as good as the owner.

   (A) as good as the owner.
   (B) good as the owner's.
   (C) good as the owner himself.
   (D) as good as those of the owner.
   (E) good like the owner's too.

24. Faster computer processors have been coming out every two months, and it has changed the way professional graphics and video editing is done.

   (A) and it has changed the way
   (B) changing the way
   (C) creating a huge change in the way that
   (D) representing a huge change in the way
   (E) having been changing the way

25. Rumor has it that Dunkin Donuts was evicted from its prime Andover location for the reason that the building's owner had a son who wanted to start up his own coffee shop.

   (A) for the reason that
   (B) because
   (C) in spite of
   (D) yet
   (E) seeing that

Improving Sentences VII

1. The dog would like to be walked, but the dog is not able to be walked by its owner.

   (A) but the dog is not able to be walked by its owner.
   (B) but the owner is not able to be walking his dog.
   (C) but its owner is not able to walk it.
   (D) and it is impossible for the owner to walk his dog.
   (E) yet the dog cannot now be walked by his owner.

2. Ma Soba, located on Chestnut Street in Boston, has the best tasting Chinese food in the city and also is reasonably priced.

   (A) and also is reasonably priced.
   (B) and also reasonable prices.
   (C) and is also of reasonable pricing.
   (D) and also reasonably priced.
   (E) and is having reasonable prices as well.

3. Like many new students, the school's complex layout baffled the Jones family for a little while toward the beginning.

   (A) the school's complex layout baffled the Jones family for a little while toward the beginning.
   (B) the Jones family was baffled by the school's complex layout at the beginning.
   (C) James Jones and his family was baffled by the school's complex layout.
   (D) James Jones and also his family were baffled by the school's complex layout, in the beginning.
   (E) James Jones and his family were baffled by the school's complex layout in the beginning.

4. The state of Hawaii consists of several small islands while being located miles off the Pacific Coast of the U.S.

   (A) while being located miles off the Pacific Coast of the U.S.
   (B) also being located miles off the Pacific Coast of the U.S.
   (C) and is located miles off the Pacific Coast of the U.S.
   (D) and it is located miles off the Pacific Coast of the U.S.
   (E) but it is located miles off the Pacific Coast of the U.S.

5. Great poetry, such as "The Raven" by Poe or the works of Longfellow, continue to be read in classrooms today.

   (A) such as "the Raven" by Poe or the works of Longfellow, continue
   (B) such as "the Raven" by Poe, or the works, of Longfellow, continue
   (C) such as "the Raven" by Poe or the works of Longfellow, continues
   (D) such as by Poe and Longfellow, "the Raven" and his works, continue
   (E) being like works by Poe and Longfellow, continues

6. The services of Beaven and Associates are always in high demand considering that his tutoring combines both excellence in teaching and a competitive market price.

   (A) considering that his tutoring combines both
   (B) seeing as how his tutoring combines both
   (C) in light of the fact that, combining
   (D) and his tutoring combines both
   (E) as his tutoring combines

7. "1776", the story of a year in the life of George Washington, fascinates many people today, being at the top of the best-seller list.

(A) today, being at the top of the best-seller list.
(B) having been top-selling on the list of today.
(C) and this is evidenced by its being on the top-seller list today.
(D) as today it is on the best-seller list
(E) being today at the top of the best-seller list.

8. Sartre, a profound philosopher, whose work almost parallels that of Nietzsche, written in the 1800's.

(A) whose work almost parallels that of Nietzsche, written in the 1800's.
(B) his work almost parallels that of Nietzsche, written in the 1800's.
(C) published works in the 1800's that almost parallel those of Nietzsche.
(D) is being almost parallel to Nietzsche's, written in the 1800's.
(E) has works that almost parallel Nietzsche's, written in the 1800's.

9. Many people are of the opinion that SUVs guzzle too much expensive gasoline, consequently, they do not buy them.

(A) gasoline, consequently, they do not buy them
(B) gasoline, and of consequence, they do not buy them
(C) gasoline, and because of this fact, they do not buy them.
(D) gasoline and consequently they are not inclined to be buying them.
(E) gasoline, and thus they do not buy them.

10. Just as computers have provided a much more efficient means of cataloging data, so fewer accountants have been hired in large businesses.

(A) so fewer accountants have been hired in large businesses.
(B) and fewer accountants have been hired in large businesses.
(C) and then fewer accounts have been being hired in large businesses.
(D) but then fewer accounts are hired in large businesses.
(E) showing that less accountants have been hired in large businesses.

11. Users of the Macintosh computer have said that it as at once more costly than the PC but still its graphics engine is more powerful.

(A) as at once more costly than the PC but still its graphics engine is
(B) is more costly than the PC, but its graphics engine is
(C) as, if not once more costly, than the PC, but its graphics engine is still
(D) at once it is more costly than the PC but it still its having a graphics engine that is
(E) once, as it cost more than the PC, but now its graphics engine is still

12. It makes little sense to close your SAT booklet while you still have ten minutes left to complete the examination.

(A) while you still have
(B) but still having
(C) when you have got
(D) and yet you have
(E) when you will have

163

13. Just because one's courses are tough <u>does not mean that you have to give up on trying all together.</u>

    (A) does not mean that you have to give up on trying all together.
    (B) does not have to mean that you are just going to give up.
    (C) does not mean that one has to give up on trying all together.
    (D) but it might still mean that you don't have to give up on trying.
    (E) but that does not mean that you have to not try at all.

14. <u>Although the Tyrannosaurus Rex is believed to have perished from the earth over 65 million years ago, its</u> remains can be found in the rural Midwest beneath the soil in fossilized form.

    (A) Although the Tyrannosaurus Rex is believed to have perished from the earth over 65 million years ago, its
    (B) Although the Tyrannosaurus Rex is believingly perished from the earth over 65 million years ago, its
    (C) Although believed to have perished over 65 million years ago, the Tyrannosaurus Rex
    (D) Because the Tyrannosaurus Rex is believed to have perished from the earth over 65 million years ago, its
    (E) In fact, the Tyrannosaurus Rex has perished from the earth over 65 million years ago, it

15. My mother always complains <u>that me screaming when my brother attacks me</u> is disruptive to her work.

    (A) that me screaming when my brother attacks me
    (B) that me screaming as my brother attacks me
    (C) that my screaming when my brother attacks me
    (D) and my screaming when my brother attacks me
    (E) when my screaming that my brother attacks me

16. <u>They say that you should wash your hands three times a day while</u> you should take a shower once a day and once after sports.

    (A) They say that you should wash your hands three times a day while
    (B) They say that you should wash your hands three times a day and
    (C) It is said that you should wash your hands three times a day while
    (D) It is said that you should wash your hands three times a day, and
    (E) It is said that you should wash your hands three times a day, but while

17. The coach, as a treat one day, decided to give a lollipop <u>to whomever wanted one.</u>

    (A) to whomever wanted one.
    (B) to whichever wanted one.
    (C) to whoever wanted one.
    (D) at whomever wanted one.
    (E) at whoever wanted one.

18. <u>The travelers coming this far, they decided</u> that they absolutely needed to finish the pilgrimage, no matter how tired they were.

    (A) The travelers coming this far, they decided
    (B) Having come this far, the travelers decided
    (C) The travelers coming this far, they decided
    (D) The travelers having came this far, they decided
    (E) Having come this far, the travelers now decide

19. Serving as both organizers and cellular telephones, <u>Blackberries, they are increasingly popular.</u>

    (A) Blackberries, they are increasingly popular.
    (B) Blackberries are becoming increasingly popular.
    (C) Blackberries, having become increasingly popular.
    (D) Blackberries were to become increasingly popular.
    (E) Blackberries are now increasingly in popularity.

20. Although only five feet in height, <u>Napoleon was a powerful and feared</u> emperor in his time.

    (A) Napoleon was a powerful and feared
    (B) Napoleon were a powerful and feared
    (C) Napoleon, powerful and feared, an
    (D) Napoleon, powerful and feared, was
    (E) Napoleon powerful and was also feared

21. The lawyer, practicing in a major Boston law firm of over 400 attorneys, <u>winning many large and important cases.</u>

    (A) winning many large and important cases.
    (B) having won many large and important cases.
    (C) has won many large and important cases.
    (D) also having won many large and important cases.
    (E) and he won many large and important cases.

22. <u>While it is important to study hard in college,</u> it is also a good idea to major in a subject of practical use in a career.

    (A) While it is important to study hard in college,
    (B) It is important to study hard in college,
    (C) While it is important to study hard in college, but
    (D) Yes, it is important to study hard in college, but
    (E) It is important to study hard in college,

23. <u>Because they work only a 35 hour work week compared with America's average 50 hour work week,</u> it is not surprising that Europe is not as economically productive.

    (A) Because they work only a 35 hour work week compared with America's average 50 hour work week,
    (B) Because it works only a 35 hour work week compared with America's average 50 hour work week,
    (C) Because Europe works only a 35 hour work week compared with America's average 50 hour work week,
    (D) Because people in Europe work only a 35 hour work week compared with America's average 50 hour work week,
    (E) Because people in Europe work only a 35 hour work week compared with people in America, who work 50 hours on average,

24. It is preposterous to assume that just because one has a speech impediment <u>as to think that he is less intelligent.</u>

    (A) as to think that he is less intelligent.
    (B) but thinking that he is less intelligent.
    (C) he has fewer intelligence.
    (D) that being less intelligent.
    (E) he is less intelligent than others.

25. Children in the 1940s read more books <u>than the 1980s or 1990s.</u>

    (A) than the 1980s or 1990s
    (B) than did the 1980s or 1990s
    (C) than they were in the 1980s or 1990s
    (D) than did children in 1980s or 1990s
    (E) then they do in the 1980s or 1990s.

Improving Sentences VIII

1. Although many citizens opposed the 5% rise in the town budget, other groups, including teachers and town officials, lobbying for it passing.

   (A) other groups, including teachers and town officials, lobbying for it passing.
   (B) other groups, including teachers and town officials, lobbied for it passing.
   (C) other citizens, including teachers and town officials, lobbying for its passing
   (D) other citizens, including teachers and town officials, lobbied for it passing.
   (E) other citizens, including teachers and town officials, lobbied for its passing.

2. The issue of child neglect, not helped at all by the presence of deadbeat dads.

   (A) neglect, not helped at all by the presence of
   (B) neglect is not helped by the presence of
   (C) neglect, not being helped at all by the presence of
   (D) neglect, not helped by the presence of
   (E) neglect had not been helped in the least by the presence of

3. Having been teased a lot as a child, Marty made sure not to ridicule anyone.

   (A) Having been teased a lot as a child, Marty
   (B) Because he was teased as a child, Marty made sure a lot
   (C) Marty was teased a lot as a child, making sure
   (D) Marty, who was often teased as a child, shall have made sure
   (E) As a child, who having been teased, Marty made sure

4. In Burma they have laws so strict that one can have your head chopped off for speeding on a city street.

   (A) they have laws so strict that one can have your head chopped off
   (B) they have laws so strict that one can have his head chopped off
   (C) they have laws so strict that one's head may be chopped off
   (D) the law is so strict that one's head may be chopped off
   (E) the law strictly enforces chopping heads off

5. Beans, like broccoli and asparagus, are green vegetables, the reason being that they contain chlorophyll, a green chemical pigment produced in photosynthesis.

   (A) Beans, like broccoli and asparagus, are green vegetables, the reason being that
   (B) Beans, similar to broccoli and asparagus, are green vegetables, the reason being that
   (C) Beans, as well like broccoli and asparagus, are green vegetables, because
   (D) Beans, like broccoli and asparagus, are green vegetables, since
   (E) Beans like broccoli and asparagus are green vegetables because

6. Both Michael Jordan and Larry Bird being recognized as masters in the field of basketball.

   (A) Both Michael Jordan and Larry Bird being recognized as masters in the area of basketball
   (B) Both Michael Jordan and Larry Bird being recognized as a master in the area of basketball
   (C) Both Michael Jordan and Larry Bird are being recognized as masters in the area of basketball
   (D) Both Michael Jordan and Larry Bird are being recognized as a master of basketball
   (E) Both Michael Jordan and Larry Bird are being recognized as masters of basketball

7. Educated in an elite prep-school it was only when I attended college that I realized how well the school had prepared me for my future academic pursuits.

   (A) Educated in an elite prep-school it was only when I attended college that I
   (B) Educated in an elite prep-school, when I
   (C) It was only when I was educated in an elite prep-school that I
   (D) Educated in an elite prep-school I
   (E) Because of my elite prep-school education, when I attended college I

8. The rationale for spending so much money for air defense is that it is an integral part of keeping our country safe from terrorists.

   (A) that it is an integral part of keeping
   (B) that air defense is being an integral part of keeping
   (C) that it is an integral part to keep
   (D) that air defense is an integral part to
   (E) to keep

9. Being that you are the better singles player, you should take on Milton's number one seed.

   (A) Being that you are the better singles player
   (B) While you are the better singles player,
   (C) With you being the better at singles,
   (D) Since you are better playing singles
   (E) Whereas you are the better singles player,

10. Seeing as how your mother is late, wouldn't it be a good use of your time to do more work, Jay?

    (A) Seeing as how your mother is late,
    (B) Because your mother is late,
    (C) Seeing your late mother,
    (D) When your mother
    (E) Seeing as much as your mother is late

11. In golf, a mulligan is when you are dissatisfied with your original shot and ask to take it over.

    (A) In golf, a mulligan is when you are
    (B) A mulligan in golf is when you are
    (C) In golf, a mulligan is a shot in which you are
    (D) A mulligan in golf is a shot in which your
    (E) A mulligan, in which you are

12. The SAT scores of any student are influenced by his natural intelligence and combined with the amount of work he puts into studying.

    (A) The SAT scores of any student are influenced by his natural intelligence and combined with
    (B) The SAT score of any student are influenced by his natural intelligence combined with
    (C) The SAT scores of any student are influenced by his natural intelligence and
    (D) The SAT score of any student are influenced by his natural intelligence and
    (E) The SAT scores of any student are influenced by his natural intelligence compounded by

13. Blaring loudly, James asked Dan to turn down the television, which was interrupting his studying.

    (A) Blaring loudly, James asked Dan to turn down the television, which was interrupting his studying.
    (B) James asked Dan to turn down the television blaring loudly, and which was interrupting his studying.
    (C) James asked Dan to turn down the blaring television, which was interrupting James's studying.
    (D) James asked Dan to turn down the television which was blaring and which was interrupting his study.
    (E) The blaring TV, interrupting James's Study, was asked to be turned off by Dan.

14. Fleas have brains the size of microscopic specks, invisible to the naked eye, which hints that they are possibly not as intelligent as humans who have brains the size of melons.

    (A) specks, invisible to the naked eye, which
    (B) specks invisible to the naked eye which
    (C) specks invisible to the naked eye that
    (D) specks, invisible to the naked eye; such a size
    (E) specks, invisible to the naked eye, in which

15. Professional paleontologists, people that study dinosaur bones, need to travel to the Midwest to find a lot of their samples.

    (A) people that study dinosaur bones, need to travel
    (B) people who study dinosaur bones, need to travel
    (C) people that study dinosaur bones, need travel
    (D) people whom study dinosaur bones, need to travel
    (E) people who study dinosaur bones, needing travel

16. The weatherman reported as to the expectability of rain this weekend as well as the possibility of much of it.

    (A) reported as to the expectability of rain this weekend as well as the possibility of much of it
    (B) said to expect a lot of rain this weekend.
    (C) reported to expect rain this weekend and expect a lot of it.
    (D) said to expect rain possibly being a lot of it.
    (E) reported that rain is to be expected in a large amount.

17. Having a good ear, recognition of melodies, as well as finger technique, Randy was able to play most any popular rock song without music.

    (A) Having a good ear, recognition of melodies, as well as finger technique, Randy was able to play most any popular rock song without music.
    (B) Without music, Randy is able to play almost any rock song because he has a good ear, recognition of melodies, as well as finger technique.
    (C) Without any music, Randy is able to play almost any rock song because he has a good ear, the ability to recognize melodies, and superb finger technique.
    (D) Randy's good ear, ability to recognize melodies, and superb finger technique allow him to play almost any popular rock song without reading music.
    (E) Without reading music, Randy can play almost any popular rock song because of his good ear, his ability to recognize melodies, and his superb finger technique.

18. The store carries everything from fruits and vegetables to junk foods and dairy products, as well as household cleaners and pet foods.

    (A) everything from fruits and vegetables to junk foods and dairy products, as well as
    (B) everything from fruits and vegetables to junk foods to dairy products, as well as
    (C) everything from fruits and vegetables to junk foods to dairy products to
    (D) many products such as fruits and vegetables, junk foods, dairy products, as well as
    (E) fruits and vegetables, junk foods, dairy products, and

19. Whether the ancient Egyptians built the great pyramids with machines or did not, they still remain one of the great wondrous feats of the world.

    (A) Whether the ancient Egyptians built the great pyramids with machines or did not, they
    (B) Whether or not the ancient Egyptians built the great pyramids with machines, they
    (C) Whether the ancient Egyptians built the great pyramids with machines or did not, it
    (D) Whether or not the ancient Egyptians built the great pyramids with machines or did not, it
    (E) Whether or not the ancient Egyptians built the great pyramids with machines, the pyramids

20. The age of 18 having been reached, Jessica decided that she wanted to go buy herself a packet of cigarettes.

    (A) The age of 18 having been reached,
    (B) Being 18 of years,
    (C) When she reached 18,
    (D) As she was 18 in terms of years,
    (E) By the years, 18,

21. During the Depression of the twenties many families found themselves starving and without money.

    (A) themselves starving and without money.
    (B) itself starving and without money.
    (C) themselves starving and being without money.
    (D) itself starving and being without money.
    (E) themselves with starvation and without money.

22. The metermaid in Andover chalks cars every hour so as to be discouraging people from violating parking laws.

    (A) so as to be discouraging
    (B) to discourage
    (C) encouraging the discouragement of
    (D) to insure
    (E) to make it unlikely

23. Because of the popularity of their ice cream in Andover, Benson's just opened a new store down the street on Rte. 28.

    (A) Because of the popularity of their ice cream in Andover,
    (B) Because of the fact that they are now so popular for ice cream in Andover,
    (C) Being so popular with ice cream in Andover, Benson's
    (D) Because it has become so popular with Andover residents,
    (E) Having been long recognized in Andover for the popularity of its ice cream

24. The Civil War was long and costly, the U.S. had to rebuild itself immediately afterward.

    (A) long and costly, the U.S. had to
    (B) long and costly, thus the U.S. had to
    (C) long and costly, and therefore the U.S. had to
    (D) yes it was long and costly, and as a result the U.S. had to
    (E) long and costly, made the U.S. having to rebuild

25. While shopping for jeans, the ones with the silver sparkles and frayed bottoms attracted Jessica's attention.

    (A) While shopping for jeans, the ones with the silver sparkles and frayed bottoms attracted Jessica's attention.
    (B) While she shopped for jeans Jessica's attention was attracted to the ones with silver sparkles and frayed bottoms.
    (C) While shopping for jeans, Jessica's attention sought the ones with silver sparkles and frayed bottoms.
    (D) While shopping for jeans, Jessica was attracted to the ones with silver sparkles and frayed bottoms.
    (E) Shopping for jeans, Jessica's attention was attracted to the ones with the silver sparkles and frayed bottoms.

Answers

Correction Symbols

case	(*nominative, possessive, objective*)	*p*	punctuation
c	capitalization	*pref*	pronoun agreement or reference
comp	improper comparison	*ros*	run-on sentence, comma splice
d	diction, wrong word, part of speech	*sp*	spelling
frag	fragment; not a sentence	*s/v*	subject ≠ verb agreement
mm	misplaced or faulty modifier	*sub*	upside down ↔ subordination
nn	double negative	*t*	tense
#	number (*singular/plural*)	*ww*	wordy, verbose, tautological
¶	paragraph		
//	parallel structure	√	ok, correct

Improving Sentences Answers I - III

Improve I	Improve II	Improve III
1. C ros	1. E comp	1. B pref
2. E ros	2. D pref	2. B ros
3. E s/v	3. C comp	3. A √
4. C pref	4. A √	4. D pref
5. B ros	5. E //	5. D #
6. D ww	6. D pref	6. C d
7. A √	7. B //	7. E comp
8. B mm	8. C mm	8. B sub
9. C pref	9. D pref	9. B pref
10. C ros	10. B mm	10. E mm
11. D comp	11. D pref	11. B #
12. E pref	12. B comp	12. B mm
13. E comp	13. D //	13. C comp
14. B mm	14. D pref	14. D ros
15. D ros	15. C ros	15. C t
16. E mm	16. C //	16. D comp
17. E mm	17. E //	17. C s/v
18. E case	18. A √	18. E ros
19. D t	19. B t	19. D ros
20. B //	20. B comp	20. A √
21. D mm	21. E t	21. E //
22. C s/v	22. B ros	22. D case
23. E #	23. C //	23. D t
24. D ros	24. D pref	24. D sub
25. A √	25. C ros	25. C //

Improving Sentences Answers IV - VI

Improve IV	Improve V	Improve VI
1. E s/v	1. C ros	1. C //
2. C //	2. B sub	2. B ros
3. B t	3. E ros	3. A √
4. E comp	4. E ros	4. B ros
5. E t	5. D mm	5. A √
6. D comp	6. B pref	6. A √
7. A √	7. B pref	7. C t
8. D t	8. C ros	8. E ros
9. D mm	9. B mm	9. A √
10. E d	10. D ros	10. B s/v
11. B comp	11. A √	11. C pref
12. D ros	12. C s/v	12. E ros
13. A √	13. A √	13. D pref
14. C //	14. C comp	14. C ros
15. C mm	15. A √	15. B pref
16. E d	16. B comp	16. D ww
17. D ros	17. B d	17. D //
18. C pref	18. C mm	18. A √
19. E ww	19. D t	19. D comp
20. A √	20. C //	20. B comp
21. C mm	21. D d	21. C pref
22. D ros	22. B d	22. E //
23. B d	23. A √	23. D comp
24. E //	24. E p	24. B pref
25. E d	25. D ros	25. B d

Improving Sentences Answers VII - VIII

Improve VII

1. C //
2. B //
3. E mm
4. C pref
5. C s/v
6. E ww
7. D mm
8. E ros
9. E ros
10. A √
11. B //
12. A √
13. C pref
14. A √
15. C case
16. D pref
17. C case
18. B t
19. B pref
20. A √
21. C ros
22. E sub
23. E comp
24. E ww
25. D comp

Improve VIII

1. E //
2. B ros
3. A √
4. D pref
5. D d
6. E ros
7. E pref
8. E ww
9. D d
10. B t
11. C pref
12. C //
13. C mm
14. D s/v
15. B pref
16. B ww
17. E //
18. E //
19. E comp
20. C t
21. A √
22. B ww
23. D pref
24. C ros
25. D mm

www.ingramcontent.com/pod-product-compliance
Lightning Source LLC
Chambersburg PA
CBHW060315240426
43661CB00059B/2770